Red Dog & Great White

Inside the America's Cup

by
Mark Clark

Byren House Publishing Inc.
New York ● Toronto

ISBN 0-920983-06-5

Library of Congress Catalog Card Number 86-071211

BYREN HOUSE PUBLISHING INC.
New York, Toronto

Book Distributor: United States
Independent Publishers Group

Book Distributor: Canada
Harcourt Brace Jovanovich
(HBJ, Canada)

Printed in Canada by
Tri-Graphic Printing Limited

Contents

Editor: Katherine Sedgwick

Cover Design & Art:
John Bianchi / Bianchi Design

Book Design:
Karen Wiens-Baltare / Artworks

Watercolors: John Bianchi

In addition to the above, I
would like to acknowledge
a special debt of gratitude
to Liz Clarke, Mary Campeau,
Kathryn MacDonald, Diane
Yocum, Edith Bramwell and
Julia Bennett.

To the many others who
contributed in the creation
of this book, from Newport,
Rhode Island to Perth,
Australia, and several points
in between, my thanks and
appreciation. —M.C.

For
Benjamin and Byron

Argosies of magic sails
Pilots of the purple twilight.
                    Tennyson

The sailing sport is an
appanage of a class of
enthusiasts who are
aristocratically concerned
with excellence at sea. For
them . . . no sacrifice is
implausible.
        William F. Buckley Jr.

A Shot Heard Around the World

A Shot Heard Around the World

If they mean to have war, let it begin here!

John Parker

It was noon. In transit across the northern hemisphere, the sun had risen to its apogee. Rhode Island Sound was ablaze with a hard brilliance, the white fire of diamonds dancing off the blue flame of a million sapphires. The late September sky had lost the hazy quality of summer: azure had given way to a blue startling in clarity as if gauze-like film had been peeled from the eye, or from the atmosphere itself. At the horizon, blazing sea met cloudless heavens—a boundary sharp and distinct, the touching point of two sovereign states of nature.

The breeze, which at dawn had been zephyrean and fickle, freshened, gusting to fifteen knots by midday. It piled the waters of the Sound onto Brenton Reef, several miles off the coast of the tiny eastern-seaboard state of Rhode Island. Inside the reef, seas were choppy and confused, seaward the Atlantic Ocean rolled inland in sweeping, foam-streaked waves.

On this pitching sea, two boats, one red-hulled, the other gleaming white like the tooth of a shark, circled one another in an apparent game of catch-as-catch-can. But it was not free-spirited gamesmanship in which they were engaged. They were drawn together by an implacable hatred born outside the bounds of an ordinary sporting contest. Alive and electric, this hatred surged across the water in dangerous high-voltage bolts. The air surrounding the warring hulls seemed ionized, explosive as gunpowder, as if sooner or later it must ignite.

The boats were powered by huge, precisely cut triangles of sail, stretched tight in the brisk wind. As their hulls cut through the gemstone sea, they left a circular wake that drifted and distended, a phosphorescent smoke ring floating on the ocean's surface.

The circle tightened as the boats drew closer together. The knife-edged bow of the aggressor, now the red boat, slashed towards the exposed stern of the other. Then, abruptly, as if by the wave of an illusionist's hand, they reversed roles; the white boat, with amazing agility, launched an attack on the red, which only at the last instant darted out of harm's way. As they vied relentlessly for the position that would give one of them the crucial edge at the start of the race to come, the mad, dangerous duel continued: red, attack . . . white, escape; white, attack . . . red, escape.

From the shoreline, along Ocean Avenue, which hugs the coves, bays and inlets south of Newport, Rhode Island, thousands of spectators squinted in the brilliant afternoon glare. Hazards and Gooseberry beaches were as crowded as on a Fourth of July weekend. At exclusive Bailey's Beach, where once John Jr. and Caroline Kennedy built sandcastles at their father's feet, spectators balanced precariously on rickety cabanas—or stood, somewhat more safely, on the roof of the low-lying clubhouse. The rocky promontories at Prices Neck and Cherry Neck, offering splendid panoramic views of Rhode Island Sound, were packed. From the Sound, the vast throng of spectators resembled a multicolored blanket of seabirds mantling an oceanside cliff.

The two boats were several miles offshore, their hulls at times almost lost beneath the horizon. But their sails, soaring more than ninety feet above deck, were clearly visible, even to the naked eye. Still, even seen through binoculars, the sails were smaller than life. Nor could the avid seaside spectators determine which boat—red or white—was the aggressor and which was the hunted. But it did not matter. Those watching the distant spectacle were drawn by the explosive atmosphere and united by a voyeuristic blood lust. For one of the boats, desperately maneuvering out there on the rim of the sky, was doomed to end this day in mortal defeat. The waters of Rhode Island Sound had become a Roman arena, the red and white boats, gladiators; and not one person, whether parked curbside on Ocean Avenue, standing on Gooseberry Beach or perched on Prices Neck, wanted to miss the moment of truth.

Above the gladiators, a rag-tag aerial circus of dozens of photographers' helicopters performed its own game of catch-as-catch-can, reminding many onlookers of a far more disquieting presence. It did not take much

Circling

imagination, particularly with the reverberating roar of dozens of rotors striking up a fearful resonance in the air, to visualize the helicopters of Vietnam. Some journalists would even frame the setting in terms of the Francis Coppola movie epic *Apocalypse Now*.

Above the helicopters, staggered at five-hundred-foot intervals, spectator aircraft flew in concentric circles. Some trailed advertising streamers that flashed bright streaks of color as if they were the fluttering tails of Chinese kites.

In the midst of the helicopters, aircraft and streamers, the Goodyear blimp floated serenely and with elephantine grace. In the air space over Rhode Island Sound, the giant silver airship had royal prerogative. For she was the eyes of the world: From her marvelous vantage point a few hundred feet above the two boats, televised pictures were being beamed to ground stations, then to satellites in orbits thousands of miles high, then earthward to other ground stations that dotted the globe. The world-wide audience for the race was estimated to be half a billion people.

On the sparkling waters of Rhode Island Sound, a vast fleet of spectator craft reminded older journalists of another era, another war. For the huge collection of pleasure craft—boats of every size and description—was this day reminiscent of the mighty armada which had steamed across the English Channel to rescue the remnants of the British expeditionary force from the debacle at Dunkirk.

The pleasure craft crowded in on the war-dance of the red boat and the white boat. Order was maintained by the U.S. Coast Guard, which had put to sea its own flotilla of cutters, buoy tenders, patrol boats and utility boats. Like sheepdogs herding an errant flock, they chased any vessel guilty of trespassing on the area of ocean reserved for the warriors.

The crews of the two boats were oblivious to the tension, excitement and general pandemonium that they generated. They continued their relentless pursuit of one another, honing to a feverish intensity their own aggressiveness.

Finally, after what seemed an eternity to sailor and spectator alike, the discharge of a cannon roared across the water. Its sharp report, at 1:05 p.m. on the 26th day of September, 1983, was heard around the world.

Another Century

1851: Race of Another Century

He is an Englishman!
For he himself has said it.

Sir William Gilbert

One hundred and thirty-two years before the race on Rhode Island Sound caught the attention—and the imagination—of the modern world, it was England, not America, that was acknowledged as the most powerful nation on earth. In 1851 America was just emerging from its infancy, having thrown off the yoke of British domination only a few generations before. Yet, in that year America gave the world a taste of what was to come when it won the Cup destined to bear her name.

Queen Victoria had occupied the British throne for the first fourteen years of a reign that would exceed six decades. During her lifetime, the sun that was Britannia would rise unequalled in the firmament of earthly powers. At its zenith, coinciding roughly with Queen Victoria's Diamond Jubilee in 1897, it would shine on one-quarter of the Earth's land mass and on one-quarter of the globe's population. The Union Jack would fly from flagstaffs rooted in the soils of Australia, New Zealand,

Burma, Ceylon, India, Arabia, much of Africa, large tracts of South America and half of North America. And from the pulpits of Westminster to the dais of Buckingham Palace, from the chambers of the House of Lords to the common rooms in London's pubs, there was talk of divinely appointed destiny.

Nineteenth-century England overflowed with imperial self-admiration. To be British was to be blessed, a sentiment widespread through every stratum of society; self-aggrandizement was a Victorian pastime. To be other than a British citizen was to be deigned ordinary. Worse still, one could be a colonial from Australia, perhaps, or Canada. But the most pitiable fate was undoubtedly that of the Americans, ex-colonials, who were viewed with condescension when considered at all. In a historical context, the achievements of the British Empire were rivaled only by those of the Romans. This suited the British well. After all, they had their Caesars, Wellington and Nelson, who had saved Europe and, in the process, civilization itself from the Corsican monster Napoleon. If there was little modesty to admire in the British, however, there was much else deserving of praise: industriousness, an indomitable spirit of adventure and exploration, ingenuity, inventiveness and a passion for excellence and progress.

So enamored of the unimpeded march of British progress was Queen Victoria's husband, Prince Albert, that he decided to put the genius of England on public display in 1851. Forgotten for the time being were the teeming slums of London, the brigades of child prostitutes, the thousands of gin mills—in general the horrors of Victorian England. Prince Albert would invite the world to see Britannia at her finest. He would hold an exhibition.

The raging productivity of the Victorians shattered nerves and punctured stomachs, but it was a thing noble, glorious, awesome in itself.

Elizabeth Hardwick

More than thirty of the world's nations accepted the Prince Consort's invitation to flaunt their genius at a world's fair. The idea of an exhibition delighted them, reflecting as it did the brotherhood of man and the emerging concept of a community of nations. Among those who would participate was a young, robust, idealistic republic, America.

The Great Exhibition was housed in a magnificent structure erected in London's Hyde Park. Dubbed the Crystal Palace, it was constructed of panes of glass that were placed to capture and reflect sunlight like a giant prism. The British were brimming with pride. The London *Times* spoke of a marriage of art, technology and something very like faith. The popular novelist Thackeray waxed poetic:

As though 'twere by a wizard's rod
a blazing arch of lucid glass
leaps like a fountain from the grass
To meet the sun!

And Queen Victoria spoke for all her subjects—and to a great extent for all civilized nations—when she described the building in her diary as "one of the wonders of the world, which England may indeed be proud of."

Under the arched roof of the glittering Crystal Palace, more than six million visitors gazed upon such an assortment of amazing and wondrous objects as had never before been seen: Daniel Gooch's marvelous locomotive *Lord of the Isles*, immaculate in green paint and polished brass, brand new from the Swindon Railway Works; hats of cabbage-tree leaves, made by Australian convicts; a dress worn by a woman soldier of the King of Dahomey; an embalmed pig from Dublin; the Koh-i-Noor diamond; and endless other oddities. Victorian England was momentarily struck dumb—first by the splendor of the Crystal Palace, then by the diversity and unimaginable fruits of man's labor and genius.

But the Victorians were never speechless for long. Theirs was an age of insatiable curiosity. After witnessing one miracle, they became impatient for the next. In due course, they turned naturally to America, a country they did not hold in any affection but about which they had an undeniable degree of inquisitiveness.

Yankee Doodle came to town
Riding on a pony.

Anonymous

The entire east end of the Crystal Palace had been reserved for American exhibits. "But what was our astonishment on arriving there," noted *Punch* magazine acidly, "to find that their contribution to the world's industry consists as yet of a few wine glasses, a square or two of soap, and a pair of salt-cellars." If England was the star of the show, America occupied the opposite end of the spectrum. The Yankees were the great disappointment of the Great Exhibition.

In fact, the Americans did send more than wine glasses and soap across the Atlantic. The McCormick Reaper, a revolutionary grain thresher, was an unqualified success, and it was predicted that it would revitalize the face of British agriculture. It did. American ingenuity had also produced the sewing machine, the electric telegraph, the rotary printing press—even the

Crystal Palace

humble but highly practical safety pin. But the products of American inventiveness somehow got lost in what amounted to a deluge of insults and derogatory abuse. Yankee-bashing became *de rigueur*. The English dailies delighted in attempting to outdo each other in belittling the American exhibits. When a certain Mr. Briggs, a renowned New York City lock picker, demonstrated his talents to a politely curious Queen Victoria, the London dailies had a field day: Mr. Briggs, they crowed with scathing wit, stole the show.

Queen Victoria herself was not above the fray, observing on one occasion the profusion of bowie knives, made entirely for Americans "who never move without one," and after another visit acerbically noting the "ludicrous" sight of two Yankees at either end of a double piano. She did, however, admit to enjoying the American minstrel show performed on the hour, every hour, during the exhibition.

Next to the McCormick Reaper, the minstrel show was the most successful of the American exhibits. Unfortunately, it summed up the prevailing and popular sentiment: A minstrel show was the high-water mark of American culture. It also reinforced another already deeply rooted Victorian prejudice—that America, their former colony, was a land populated by crude, albeit clever, peasants. The label "Yankee" remained synonymous with low birth and cunning.

America could be forgiven if she was a little bit lost at England's Great Exhibition, a little in awe of the august company in which she found herself. As a nation she was not yet tightly stitched at the seams. Still ahead was the devastation of civil war. She had not yet attained her vision of nationhood—a union of states from sea to shining sea. Yet, at the eleventh hour Yankee pride was to be restored. The knight in shining armor was an unexpected and unheralded champion: a racing yacht bearing a name destined to live in glory—*America*.

And guardian angels sung this strain:
Rule, Britannia, rule the waves.

James Thomson

Britannia owed her far-flung empire to her command of the world's seas. As a maritime power she was historically without peer. From Drake's defeat of the Spanish Armada in the sixteenth century to Nelson's defeat of the French at Trafalgar over two hundred years later, no country could equal the force of the British Navy. An island realm, England was endowed with seamen and shipbuilders of instinct and genius.

Her many seafaring explorers—Cooke, Wallace, Franklin, even William Bligh of undying *Bounty* fame and Charles Darwin on board H.M.S. *Beagle*—charted the oceans and lands of every continent from the Galápagos, Tierra del Fuego and Hawaii, to Hudson Bay on the Arctic Circle and Cape Ann in Antarctica. By Victoria's reign, her merchant fleet was the world's largest. Her trade routes encircled the globe, pole to pole, tropic to tropic. At London, the Thames waterfront was a thicket of masts, spars and rigging, with hundreds of ships docked; others by the dozen rode the tide, waiting their turn to relinquish cargoes from every corner of the British Empire and the world beyond.

But in the shipyards of New England and down the length of the Eastern seaboard, particularly in Boston, Baltimore and New York, seafaring genius was also at work. The American talent was led by the likes of Donald McKay, an expatriate Nova Scotian by whom the fastest ships afloat were being designed. Nothing constructed in the venerable shipyards of the British Isles on the rivers Clyde or Mersey or in the dockyards of Southampton or Belfast, could compare.

McKay created the magnificent clipper ship, the *ne plus ultra* of the sailing vessel. In his *Oxford History of the American People*, Samuel Eliot Morison observes: "These clipper ships of the early 1850s were built of wood in shipyards from Rockland in Maine to Baltimore. These architects, like poets who transmute nature's message into song, obeyed what wind and wave had taught them, to create the noblest of all sailing vessels, and the most beautiful creations of man in America. With no extraneous ornament except a figurehead, a bit of carving and a few lines of gold leaf, their one purpose of speed over the great ocean routes was achieved by perfect balance of spars and sails to the curving lines of the smooth black hull; and this harmony of mass, form and color was practiced to the music of dancing waves and of brave winds whistling in the rigging."

The very names of the great clippers were meant to signal their nobility and gallantry and their worship of the demon-god speed: *Rapid*, *Lightning*, *Witchcraft*, *Challenge*, *Sovereign of the Seas*, *Great Republic*, *Champion of the Seas*. But speed for speed's sake was not the important thing. What made the clipper ships so valuable was the role they could play in the world of commerce. It was an era when many vast fortunes were made, and these swift ships were often crucial to the process.

The link between commerce and the clipper was gold. Overnight, gold could make a poor man rich and a rich man richer, and the nineteenth century was marked by recurrent epidemics of gold fever. When the fever struck, few were immune. Rational thought and caution were thrown to the wind and replaced by an intense and passionate lust that could only be assuaged by a pilgrimage to the gold fields. The difficulty lay in the location of these fields: Australia and California. Australia lay half a world away, across the length and breadth of at least two oceans. A clipper bound from New York to Sydney was confronted with two routes: south down the length of the Atlantic to Cape Horn, then west across the Pacific; or southeast across the Indian Ocean. New York to San Francisco was only slightly less perilous a voyage: down the Atlantic coastline of South America and, after rounding Cape Horn, north up the Pacific coast. The journey overland was a dangerous and back-breaking purgatory of several months' duration. A man suffering from gold fever did not have several months. He measured his time in days, as carefully as if they were his last days on this earth. The angel that carried him to his Elysian Fields was the clipper ship.

They did not look like money-making machines. Caught under full sail at sunrise, they resembled billowing, roseate sea clouds climbing and brushing against the shimmer of morning stars. But their sails flew on the wind; they were waterborne wings of Mercury and literally gave wing to commerce. New York to San Francisco, via the dreaded Cape Horn, was a distance of more than eight thousand miles. The clipper *Flying Cloud* made the trip on her maiden voyage in an astonishing eighty-nine days. The *James Baines* set a record of twelve and a half days from Boston to Liverpool, then sailed on to Melbourne, Australia—via the Cape of Good Hope and the wind-swept latitudes known by sailors the world over as the roaring forties—in a record time of sixty-three days. Its total journey: more than twelve thousand sea miles.

There were other areas of marine enterprise in which America flourished. Some were noble; others were not. For decades African slaves had been transported via the notorious Middle Passage, although trafficking was against international marine law. The Royal Navy was no match for the insufferable but superb American seamen who brought slaves to their country. Once on the high seas, the Americans simply outfoxed and outraced the long arm of the British navy, and with unsurpassed cheek. *Wanderer*, originally a pleasure yacht owned by a Georgia slaving syndicate—which flew the burgee of the New York Yacht Club—once entertained the captain and officers of a royal navy brigantine anchored alongside. Even as the dinner table was being cleared, seven hundred and fifty slaves were surreptitiously packed below deck and, before the astonished eyes of Her Majesty's navy, the ship set sail for America.

Towering genius disdains a beaten path.
It seeks regions hitherto unexplored.

Abraham Lincoln

There were other, more laudable seafaring endeavors to America's credit, though only a few could rival the breakthrough in ship design of the clipper. One of the more praiseworthy American ventures was the New York pilot schooner, designed to navigate the notoriously treacherous tides and currents in the Hudson estuary at the mouth of New York Harbor. The schooner proved to be one of the fastest, most maneuverable ships ever to set sail. Its designer, George Steers, had discarded the traditional English lines, described as a "cod's head and mackerel tail," for a long, sharp bow, an arrowhead that sliced through waves rather than bludgeoning forward by brute force.

In 1850 industrialist John Cox Stevens, impressed with Steers, commissioned him to design a yacht faster than any on the seas. That yacht was to be *America*.

Steers took the best from his pilot schooners and borrowed unabashedly from the sharply raked lines of the clipper ship. The result was a boat that fairly glided over the water. She became known as an "out-and-outer"—a thoroughbred built for speed and speed alone.

Like his father, a Revolutionary War colonel-*cum*-entrepreneur, John Cox Stevens amassed enormous wealth in the booming economy of the newly industralized northern states. His holdings were extensive and varied: New York real estate, railroads, shipping and even an amusement park in Hoboken, New Jersey. Like others in the emerging *nouveau riche* American aristocracy, Stevens played as hard as he worked, and when he played, money was no object. Among his leisure pursuits—in addition to more than a passing interest in horse racing—was a passion for sailing. But his yachts, like his horses, were bred for the race course.

In John Cox Stevens beat the heart of a natural-born competitor. He demanded excellence of George Steers and fully expected *America* to surpass anything on the water. He was one of the first in a bloodline of ardent American risk takers—men like Cornelius Vanderbilt (patriarch of American yachting society), Leonard Jerome (grandfather of Winston Churchill and one of the founders of horse racing's Jockey Club), Joseph P. Kennedy (father of a president) and modern-day broadcasting magnate Ted Turner—who wished to excel in every endeavor and frequently succeeded. Stevens intended the schooner to cross the Atlantic, there to take on the best racing yachts the British could muster. When it came to England, Stevens suffered no inferiority complex. He issued an open challenge to the Royal Yacht Squadron, the world's oldest and most elite yacht club.

Steven's challenge was in the best sporting tradition and completely in keeping with the ostensible spirit of the Great Exhibition: the sharing of a nation's genius, in this instance shipbuilding and design, with the rest of the world. The Earl of Wilton, commodore of the Royal Yacht Squadron, responded in kind: "For myself I may be permitted to say that I shall have great pleasure in extending to your countrymen any civility that lies in my power and shall be glad to avail myself of any improvements in shipbuilding that the industry and skill of your nation have enabled you to elaborate."

During the summer of 1851, *America* crossed the Atlantic to Le Havre, France. There the schooner received a new coat of glistening black paint before proceeding to England, which she reached at the end of July. The Royal Yacht Squadron was then, as it is now, located at Cowes on the Isle of Wight, which lies a few miles off the south coast of England. Founded in 1815, the squadron is housed in a castle built by Henry VIII.

To escape the oppressive humidity of a London August, it was the custom of Queen Victoria and her retinue to retire to Osborne House near Cowes. The Cowes season, in fact, heralded the end of the London season. Cowes is as pretty as a postcard, an idyllic village on the north coast of Wight. The entire island is charming, known for its rocky promontories, multi-colored sand cliffs, chalk hills and immaculate and verdant gardens. It was here that Queen Victoria spent her youth, and it was here that she would return to die.

During the first week of August, the Royal Yacht Squadron staged regattas of such magnificence that the sleepy Isle of Wight was transformed into the social center for Europe's upper classes. The Cowes season would be the precursor to America's Cup summers in Newport, Rhode Island.

Stevens' decision to take on the British met with considerable public antagonism at home. The outspoken Horace Greeley, founder and editor of the *New York Tribune* and twenty years later an unsuccessful can-

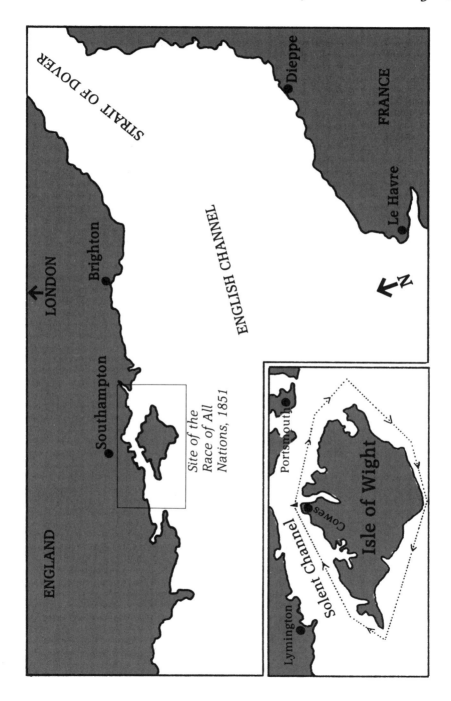

STRAIT OF DOVER

Dieppe

FRANCE

Le Havre

LONDON

Brighton

ENGLISH CHANNEL

N

Southampton

Site of the
Race of All
Nations, 1851

ENGLAND

Portsmouth

Isle of Wight

Cowes

Solent Channel

Lymington

didate for the U.S. presidency warned, "The eyes of the world are on you. You will be beaten, and the country will be abused, as it has been in connection with the Great Exhibition." Fearful of the outcome, he implored Stevens not to race against any British yachts. Greeley's fears were shared by the American ambassador to Paris, William Rives. Invoking his office, Rives virtually ordered Stevens not to race and inflict further injury on an already savaged American image. But Stevens' daring arrogance was worthy even of the British aristocracy, and he blithely ignored the ambassador, the future presidential candidate and the other nay sayers. He knew, as they could not, the ground, or rather the deck, on which he stood.

Stevens' confidence appeared well founded. When his ship dropped anchor in the Solent, the narrow channel between the Isle of Wight and the mainland, she immediately set tongues wagging—and put fear into the hearts of Royal Yacht Squadron members. Nothing quite like her had been seen before. The press described her as a "rakish looking craft" and, in less romantic terms, simply as "suspicious looking." The English sailing establishment flocked to inspect her. They were led by the Royal Yacht Squadron's most eminent member, the aging Marquis of Anglesey. The Marquis was a blunt-spoken sportsman of whom it was said, "He is typical of his generation: hard-living, hard-riding and hard-swearing, and yet kind-hearted and extremely hospitable." Missing a leg from the battle of Waterloo forty years before, he stumped around the deck of *America* on his peg leg and muttered a famous prophecy: "If she is right, then all of us are wrong." The Marquis, knowingly or unknowingly, had touched a raw nerve. No one, least of all the Royal Yacht Squadron, wanted to race the Yankee yacht. Even the nearby Royal Victoria Yacht Club, a cut below the prestigious

Squadron, would not allow her to enter its annual regatta because she was owned not by a single gentleman but by a business-like syndicate.

This fine point of etiquette infuriated John Cox Stevens. He was steadfast in his resolve to beat the British at their own game. He threw down a gauntlet that, he reasoned, could surely not be ignored. He offered the astronomical sum of ten thousand pounds (today worth perhaps half a million dollars) to any yacht that could beat *America*. The gauntlet drew not a single challenger. The London *Times* showed its undisguised admiration of Stevens' audacious challenge and, dismayed at the uncharacteristic lack of "pith and courage" displayed by its countrymen, compared them with a flock of pigeons paralyzed by fear of a marauding hawk.

Such steely barbs stung the Royal Yacht Squadron. The ten-thousand-pound challenge died a natural death for lack of takers. But the squadron did invite *America* to compete in its fourth annual race around the Isle of Wight, a distance of fifty-three miles. The prize was the Hundred Guinea Cup, matter-of-factly named after its price tag.

'Twas a famous victory.

Robert Southey

It was publicized as the Race of All Nations despite there being but two countries entered. This was, after all, the nineteenth century, age of the grandiloquent pronouncement. The contest for the Hundred Guinea Cup was set for August 22nd. England would be represented by her fifteen fastest yachts. Their sole opposition: *America*.

The buildup to the race was feverish. The London *Times* dispatched a special correspondent to cover local color and, of course, the race itself. On August 20th he reported, "The anxiety attending this race is deep and earnest." The local old salts, of whom there were many (including a number from the nearby ports of Southampton, Portsmouth and Lymington), predicted defeat for the home side despite overwhelming superiority in numbers. But there was an important factor favoring the British. The Isle of Wight is surrounded by treacherous shoals and subject to wind conditions charitably described by visiting sailors as idiosyncratic. The tides and currents are also strong and not always predictable. Knowledge of local waters is invaluable, if not indispensable. A ship caught in a wind-hole and facing a strong headtide can find itself not only drifting backwards, it can also end up on a rocky shoal with disastrous consequences. The sailors of the Royal Yacht Squadron were on intimate terms with these local conditions. The Americans were forced to rely on an English pilot who, in an anonymous letter to Stevens, was accused of being in league with his countrymen. These disadvantages notwithstanding, *America* was a popular underdog. She had pith, and the seafarers among those crowding the esplanade, the beaches and the rooftops of Cowes knew an out-and-outer when they saw one.

The fateful day dawned bright and clear and, to Stevens' profound relief, with brisk sea breezes. The industrialist, who was aboard ship, had secret misgivings that *America* would be slow in light air. Promptly at ten o'clock, off the porch of the Royal Yacht Squadron's castle, the start of the race was sounded.

America made an inauspicious beginning, hoisting her sails before she raised her anchor. She floundered awkwardly around her anchor cable in several moments of unseamanlike disarray only to avoid—narrowly—

America·1851

collision with a packed spectator steamer. The result was that *America* got off dead last. Then the wind dropped and the tide turned against her. The British yachts, which drew less water and knew where the tide pulled less insistently, began to outpace the American yacht.

The fears of Greeley and Rives suddenly appeared well founded. *America* would succeed only in splattering more egg on the face of the United States of America. But Stevens was not unduly alarmed. He knew the tides must turn and the capricious wind wane, then gain in strength. He was right. The wind picked up, and quite suddenly *America* gathered momentum. Her speed astonished her British rivals. The squadron yachts drew up in formation. They formed a solid wall of sail, a barrier to the onrush of the rapidly gaining *America*. Come hell or high water they were determined to thwart the advance of the Yankee upstart. Fair play be damned; America and England were again at war—this time on Britannia's home ground.

The Yankee schooner was not intimidated. *America* slipped into the ranks of the British fleet and nimbly navigated around eleven of the squadron yachts, leaving them gasping for breath in her windshadow. In a matter of moments she had moved from last to fifth, a mere two minutes behind the leader, *Volante*, with the threesome of *Freak*, *Aurora* and *Gypsy Queen* between. Neck and neck, the five yachts beat around the eastern extremity of Wight and began the long windward passage down the length of her seaward south coast.

Stevens' schooner *America* headed into the wind as if shot from a cannon. The *Times* correspondent could scarcely believe his eyes: "Her canvas was as flat as a sheet of paper," he reported incredulously. "While the cutters were thrashing through the water, sending the spray over their bows, and the schooners were wet up to the foot of the foremast, *America* was as dry as a bone." *America* was like a projectile skimming the surface of the English Channel. Her opponents, the proud and mighty ships of the Royal Yacht Squadron, were left to taste the bitter spray of salt she so disdainfully flung back in their faces. But it was only half past eleven in the morning, the race barely an hour and a half old.

Shortly before one o'clock while laboring against the onslaught of wind and a strong current, *America* snapped a boom. Potential disaster lay at her foot. Stevens' crew set to work as though possessed. The repairs consumed half a nerve-wracking hour, yet so commanding was her lead that no competitor approached within a mile.

By midafternoon, the race was half over and *America's* lead was fully two and a half miles. By five-thirty she had stretched her lead to an astounding seven miles. Finally, at eight o'clock, in the dying light and in a dying breeze, she ghosted past Cowes, the Royal Yacht Squadron castle and the Royal yacht *Victoria and Albert*. On board was Queen Victoria, uncertain of the identity of the winning yacht. Certainly she could be forgiven for assuming it was English. After all, Britannia, not America, ruled the waves. And as *America* sailed past in the waning light, her crew doffed hats and stood, as a mark of respect, for several moments with uncovered heads. Perhaps some of the spectators were surprised to see such a posture of fealty from a crew of Yankees and republicans.

"Who is first?" Queen Victoria is reported to have inquired.

"*America*, your Majesty."

A lengthy pause is said to have followed this response.

"And who is second?"

"Madam, there is no second," is the

apocryphal reply.

The truth of the matter is that the nearest English competitor was but minutes behind *America*. The smallest vessel in the race, the cutter *Aurora*, had closed the gap in the dying wind with a marvelous last-leg dash. Given another half hour, she might well have caught *America* and rewritten history. But on the crowded sweeping lawns of the Royal Yacht Squadron castle, in its hallowed rooms and on the decks of the defeated yachts, there was mortification. *America*'s victory stunned not just the English yachting establishment; it staggered the arrogance and complacency of Britannia herself.

The Race of all Nations was more than a yacht race. *America*'s victory challenged Britain's command of the high seas—challenged, symbolically, the British Empire. The implications of America's growing prowess at sea, reinforced by Stevens' daring gambit, were profound and disquieting to the upper levels of English society and government. A new sun was rising. A prescient London newspaper intoned: "We write to record our opinion that the empire of the seas must before long be ceded to America; its persevering enterprise, its great commerce, are certain to secure this prize; nor will England be in a condition to dispute it with her. America, as mistress of the ocean, must overstride the civilized world."

At first the British were less than gracious in defeat, although Queen Victoria herself could not have been more magnanimous. She came aboard *America* and presented each crew member with a gold sovereign. Others suggested the yacht had won by unfair and nefarious means. The ship was, after all, crewed by Yankees of low cunning. A propeller was suspected, as was propulsion by means of a hidden steam engine. This was poor sportsmanship, characteristic of a vengeful Goliath, nose bloodied by a stone fired over the waves from a slingshot in the hand of a young David.

The ridicule that had been heaped upon America at the Great Exhibition was, to say the least, equalized by *America*'s victory. England had been humbled in her own element. After the debacle at the Crystal Palace, Daniel Webster could be forgiven his euphoric and triumphant proclamation about the race, uttered in a speech to the Massachusetts House of Representatives: "Like Jupiter among the gods, America is first and there is no second." From Paris came a letter positively effusive with praise: "To beat Britannia, 'whose flag has braved a thousand years the battle and the breeze,' to beat her in her own native seas, in the presence of her Queen, and contending against a fleet of fifteen sail of her picked models of naval architecture, owned and personally directed by the proudest names of her nobility—her Marlboroughs and her Angleseys—is something that may well encourage us in the race of maritime competition which is set before us." The author? None other than Ambassador William Rives, who but a few weeks earlier had pleaded with Stevens not to engage Britannia on the sea.

Why had *America* won? Partly because of superior technology. Her sails were made of Colt's cotton duck, which held the wind much better than traditional English flax. But she also owed victory to her brilliant designer. When he created *America*, George Steers was only thirty. He was not tied to convention or blinded by the orthodox. He stepped out on a tightrope of daring new concepts, not afraid of the fall if he failed.

Then there were John Cox Stevens and his syndicate.

These men were the new Americans, the first in the lineage of great entrepreneurs—a lineage that continues unbroken from that era to this day. They believed in themselves and they believed in the greatness of their country. They demanded not simply a fast yacht but the fastest yacht in the world, and they got it. They didn't give a damn about the supposedly unbeatable English or the shimmering Crystal Palace that rose out of Hyde Park. They threw a giant shadow on the Palace and on the empire it represented.

Hail, Columbia! happy land!
Hail ye heroes! heaven-born band!

Joseph Hopkinson

The heroes returned to New York—minus *America*. That gallant ship was dispassionately sold within a month of her glorious victory to Lord John de Blaquière, an Irish peer. She survived for almost a century, passing from owner to owner. In 1942 she met an ignominious end, destroyed by the collapse of the boatshed in which she was sheltered.

Upon their return, Stevens and his fellow syndicate members were the toast of the town. New York greeted them like returning conquerors: "Our Modern Argonauts: They have brought home, not the Golden Fleece, but that which gold cannot buy, National Renown."

The Hundred Guinea Cup became the America's Cup. It was passed from house to house by syndicate members. There was talk of melting it down into souvenir medals that would be given to grandchildren as precious keepsakes. But another idea surfaced and was adopted.

In 1857, the Cup was bestowed upon the New York

Yacht Club as the prize for an international competition. The Deed of Gift specified: "It is to be distinctly understood that the Cup is to be the property of the club, and not of the members thereof, or owners of the vessel winning it in the match." The New York Yacht Club then advised seven yacht clubs in seven countries of the new competition and promised "a liberal, hearty welcome, and the strictest fair play."

For one hundred and thirty-two years—the longest winning record in the history of sport—the America's Cup remained in the possession of the New York Yacht Club. Whether or not challengers were given a "liberal, hearty welcome" and treated to "the strictest fair play" has been a moot point in the intervening decades. Regardless, by 1983 the New York Yacht Club had fielded twenty-four challenges since acquiring the Cup almost a century and half earlier, winning every one. A total of ninety-five races had been run, in the early years in New York Harbor, then off Newport on Rhode Island Sound. The American defenders won eighty-nine of those races and lost but six.

In 1983, the New York Yacht Club faced its twenty-fifth defense. The challengers were from a land with a population of a mere fifteen million—a handful compared with America's hundreds of millions. It was a flashback to 1851, when David was America, Goliath the British Empire. Now Australia was David, and America the Goliath of the twentieth century. There was genius at work in the shipyards of faraway Australia, in places like Sydney, Melbourne and Perth —as there had been in the last century in Boston, Baltimore and New York and before that at the great shipbuilding centers on the rivers Clyde and Mersey and the Belfast Lough. Would the summer of 1983 be as much a portent of the future as the summer of 1851?

1983: The Twenty-fifth Defense

Dramatis Personae

The American Defense

Liberty . . . . *Red Dog*
The New York Yacht Club

Dennis Conner . . . . Helmsman of *Liberty*
Johan Valentijn . . . . Designer of *Liberty*
Ed du Moulin . . . . *Liberty* syndicate chief

The crew of *Red Dog* . . . .

> Tom Whidden, Halsey Herreshoff, Bob Campbell, Kyle Smith, John Marshall, John Wright, Scott Vogel, Tom Rich, Eddie Trevelyan, John Hufnagel

The Australian Challenge

Australia II . . . . *Great White*
The Royal Perth Yacht Club

John Bertrand . . . . Helmsman of *Australia II*
Ben Lexcen . . . . Designer of *Australia II*
Alan Bond . . . . *Australia II* syndicate owner

The crew of *Great White* . . . .

> Hugh Treharne, Grant Simmer, Colin Beashel, Skip Lissiman, John Longley, Brian Richardson, Ken Judge, Phil Smidmore, Peter Costello, Damian Fewster

1:05 pm

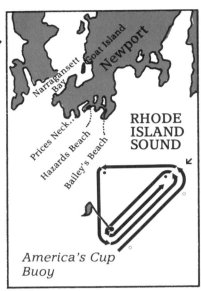

Narragansett Bay

Goat Island

Newport

Prices Neck

Hazards Beach

Bailey's Beach

RHODE ISLAND SOUND

America's Cup Buoy

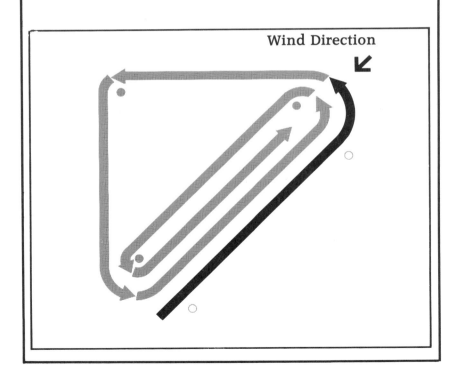

Wind Direction

The First Leg

The race is to the swift;
The battle to the strong.

John Davidson

The cannon roars. The smoke from the blast eddies skyward, hovers for an instant, is seized by the wind and flung back toward the two advancing arrows of red and white. Seconds earlier the boats had ended their circling war-dance on the waters of Rhode Island Sound and, on roughly parallel tracks, darted for the start-line. Now the bow of the red boat neatly slices the veil of thin, vanishing smoke. She draws first blood; as in four of her six previous encounters with the white boat, she has crossed the start-line ahead.

It is September 26, 1983, and race seven has begun. Overhead, from the gondola attached to the underbelly of the Goodyear blimp, word is flashed to the world: *Liberty* wins start by eight seconds. Eight seconds. A boat length, fifty to sixty precious feet; it seems a substantial lead.

At the bottom of the world, fully a hemisphere away, Australia can almost be heard to groan. But here on the Sound, beneath the Indian-summer sun, the American spectator fleet blows horns, whistles and claxons for *Liberty*. Most of the spectators remain tight-lipped, however. For *Australia II* has lost starts before and still come back to claim victory. In the fifth race of this best-of-seven competition, for instance, she was behind by a whopping thirty-seven seconds at the start-line: In just over half a minute the red boat was the owner of a seventy-five yard lead. With the Americans leading the match three races to one at that point, a victory in race five would have given them the America's Cup. But *Australia II* came back from the dead; the Australians fought off the American assault and went on to win the race.

Over the long course of an America's Cup race, eight seconds is not a secure lead. On top of that, the boat that wins a start measured against time may be the loser measured against distance. For unlike the start of a hundred-yard dash, a sailing race's start-line is rarely parallel to the finish line. The America's Cup start-line is an imaginary line between a buoy and the New York Yacht Club's race committee motor launch, *Black Knight*, which is affected by currents, tides and wind. As a result, racers crossing the line may find themselves advantageously or disadvantageously positioned—depending on the angle of their crossing—in relation to the buoy that marks the end of the First Leg.

And there is another factor to take into account: momentum. One boat may have more wind than another and, even though it crosses

Converging

the start-line behind, it may be driving forward at greater speed. This is exactly what has happened to *Australia II* on this day. It crosses the line eight seconds behind *Liberty* but with both position and momentum in its favor. The Australian boat eats up the seconds that separate it from the American.

The start is quickly re-assessed by the broadcasters: *Australia II*, having started eight seconds behind *Liberty*, has captured the lead.

Australia exhales with relief; America holds her breath.

Australia II has captured the lead . . . .

It is now several minutes into the first leg of the all-important race. The two 12-Meters, sailing into the wind, must tack—change course by sixty to seventy degrees. They will converge and cross each other's paths. There is silence on the water and on the boats themselves. This is a moment of truth, a turning point, that may establish a new leader.

On they rush at each other, smacking through the choppy waves. Hearts pound; adrenaline surges. Photographers are poised, hanging precariously from open helicopter doors and ignoring the stomach-lurching aerobatics of their pilots, who are jockeying for position.

Suddenly the suspense is over. The two boats have avoided what appeared to be a certain, horrendous collision. *Australia II* has crossed ahead—two full boat lengths in front of *Liberty*.

The wakes of the two combatants intersect to form a giant, foaming X. It lasts but a second before it is absorbed by the hard blue ocean.

Now breath is taken, hearts slow. On board the Australian observer yacht, a spark of euphoria is quickly subdued. The race is barely half an hour old; there are more than twenty miles yet to sail. And yachtsmen, like all ocean sailors, are a superstitious breed. There is no wish to tempt the gods of wind and sea into playing a cruel trick on those with premature visions of victory. Still, the facial muscles of Alan Bond, syndicate owner of *Australia II*, and Ben Lexcen, designer of the Australian boat, cannot help creasing in a fleeting but heartfelt smile.

On board the official American observer craft, panic rises in a dozen throats. Bob McCullough, Bus Mosbacher, Briggs Cunningham and Bob Bavier—all former Cup defenders—have never experienced even a foretaste of defeat. Some spectators on board retreat below deck to swallow a stiff drink to revive spirits, courage and hope.

Man can will nothing unless he has first understood that he must count on no one but himself.   *Sartre*

Racing yachts, as do most sailboats, invariably manifest preferences as to wind and its direction. Some sail better upwind or to weather; others are at home in downwind conditions. In this regard racing yachts are not unlike thoroughbred racehorses, some of which prefer wet to dry track. The ideal 12-Meter, like the ideal Triple Crown thoroughbred, operates at peak performance regardless of wind or track. Racing yachts resemble racehorses in another way: Both can be highly temperamental, possessed of idiosyncratic personalities. Some 12-Meters love stiff sea breezes—in the fifteen to twenty-five knot range. Others are the opposite, performing best in light winds. A winning 12-Meter helmsman must possess the sure hands and instinct of a champion jockey.

Dennis Conner, helmsman for the American defender *Liberty*, had proved time and again that he possessed such attributes. But then, never until this summer had he had such a fight on his hands, and *Liberty* was wayward in upwind seas. In five out of six previous encounters with *Australia II*, his crew had been bettered on the first leg. In race three, *Liberty* had rounded the first mark a full minute behind; and in race six, she had trailed by more than two minutes. *Australia II* had gone on to win both races by commanding margins.

Conner knows he must reverse *Liberty*'s tendency to fall behind during the early upwind leg of this race if he hopes to go on to claim ultimate victory. For he is confronted not only with his own boat's upwind weakness but with *Australia II*'s unassailable superiority during the downwind run. Granted, that run lies some fifteen sailing miles distant—four legs, to be exact. But two of those four legs are upwind; they pander to *Australia II*'s strength and prey on *Liberty*'s Achilles heel. Thus Conner, although the race is but minutes old, must find a way to neutralize the white boat's upwind advantage. He will not be permitted a single defensive posture. He will have to be on the offensive, ever aggressive, ever alert, to exploit any sudden opening offered by the Australians.

At a respectful distance the spectator fleet follows the two argonauts, their progress constantly monitored by the Coast Guard. Inside the Coast Guard cordon, a small fleet of perhaps thirty motor boats is permitted to encroach on the race course. These include the international press corps boat and vessels carrying privileged members of the New York Yacht Club, as well as motor yachts belonging to the other eight syndicates that have competed in the elimination series over the course of the long summer months.

Two within this elite group are elevated to further status: *Black Swan*, belonging to Alan Bond, owner of the white boat; and *Fox Hunter II*, which carries the New York Yacht Club America's Cup committee. Committee members are impeccably attired in blazers and straw boaters; many wear slacks which match the red hull of their warrior. These are the men who have passed the torch of victory—the torch that has burned brightly for one hundred and thirty-two years—to Dennis Conner.

Among the former Cup defenders on board *Fox Hunter II* is Briggs Cunningham. He skippered *Columbia* in 1958 when competition for the Cup resumed after a twenty-one year hiatus, due in part to World War II and in part to the enormous cost of building the huge racing yachts of that era.

In 1958, Cunningham and *Columbia* defended the Cup against *Sceptre*, of Great Britain's Royal Yacht Squadron. It proved to be a case of *nolo contendere*—a replay of *America*'s victory of just over a century before. *Columbia* had been match-hard, having raced all summer against tough competitors who, like her, wanted the right to carry America's colors into the Cup defense. Cunningham's toughest opponent was *Vim*, skippered by fellow committee member Emil "Bus" Mosbacher Jr. *Vim* and *Columbia* slugged it out all summer long. The average margin of victory was a scant thirty-two seconds, but ultimately *Vim* proved herself to be a light-air boat. The summer of 1958 brought brisk breezes with which *Columbia* proved more at home, and so the right to defend the Cup went to Briggs Cunningham.

Columbia was everything *Sceptre* was not: A product of the legendary American designer Olin Stephens, she was sleek and sharp, her rigging aerodynamically refined, her sails state-of-the-art. She routed *Sceptre* in four straight races.

Also on board *Fox Hunter II* during this final 1983 race was Bob Bavier, who, with *Constellation*, defended the Cup in 1964 against the British challenger *Sovereign*. Three other members of the 1983 America's Cup committee, Robert McCullough (chairman), Victor Romagna and Stanley Livingston, although not defending helmsmen, were all 12-Meter veterans. Each of these men is a yachtsman to the bone, familiar with the bottom line in America's Cup racing: winning.

As they watch this critical race, the faces of these men are grim. They imagine themselves in the cockpit of *Liberty*, in the shoes of Dennis Conner. To a man, by sheer force of will, they attempt to fill her sails, powering her far ahead of *Australia II*. For they know that the red boat, whether victor or vanquished, will sip from the cup of immortality. But will the taste be sweet victory or bitter defeat? That answer will come before the

September sun sets in the western sky. In the interim, these proud, dignified men stand or sit or, unable to contain their energy, pace the decks and passageways of *Fox Hunter II*—each experiencing private moments of agony.

On board the American defender, Dennis Conner has no time for despair. If he loses, there will be time enough for that. It is almost unthinkable that he might be the first American to lose the America's Cup after almost a century and a half of continuous victory. But the glorious careers of his predecessors on *Fox Hunter II* are a shadow on his heart.

Forgotten is the fact that until thirteen days ago he, Dennis Conner, stood with them as an equal. He had defeated *Australia* in 1980 with *Freedom*, winning the match four races to one. But that did not satisfy him. Instead, it reshaped his ambition: to defend successfully at least three America's Cup challenges. That would put him on the same pedestal as the legendary Harold "Mike" Vanderbilt, who won all three Depression-era matches (with *Enterprise*, 1930; *Rainbow*, 1934; and *Ranger*, 1937). Vanderbilt's America's Cup record was unprecedented: twelve races won, only two lost. When the dust of the 1980 campaign settled, Conner decided to better that record.

So at the outset of the summer of 1983 he could not afford a single loss. But that goal was rudely uprooted thanks to *Australia II*. The white boat had beaten him three times already—the best record against a defender in America's Cup history. And in one of those races, the third, she won by three minutes, fourteen seconds, the greatest margin of victory ever by a challenger. The previous record, two minutes, forty-seven seconds, was a half-century old. It belonged to Britain's *Endeavour*, which took those two 1934 races from Mike Vanderbilt's otherwise perfect score card. *Australia II* had then beaten her own record in the sixth race, winning by three minutes, twenty-five seconds. But for Conner the worst so far had been the first attempt at race three. The Australian lead had been an astounding five minutes, fifty-seven seconds—almost six hundred yards, or thirty boat lengths. After five hours and fifteen minutes in a dying breeze, the race had been called. For Dennis Conner, the reprieve had been a godsend.

Australia II has crossed ahead....

Conner steals a look at *Australia II*, one hundred yards ahead. The Australian sails—superbly cut by Tom Schnackenberg, a New Zealander recognized as a top craftsman in his field—are taut against the wind. With Schnackenberg's sails and Ben Lexcen's design, *Australia II* appears to be the embodiment of genius. And *Liberty*...could she be obsolete?

But Conner is not about to roll over and play dead. At that moment, he senses a sudden uplift of the wind filling the boat with power. The red hull tucks into the water as if it were a skier crouched to reduce wind resistance. As *Liberty* begins to shoot forward, thoughts of *Fox Hunter II* and her distinguished passengers are banished from Conner's mind.

On board *Australia II*, helmsman John Bertrand hears the ominous news from his tactician, Hugh Treharne: The American boat is gaining ground. In the last two races, the fifth and sixth, the Australian boat was able to find the wind and steal the victory. Today's race seems to be a reversal of that trend.

Red Dog & Great White

The poet's pen ... gives to airy nothing
A local habitation and a name.   Shakespeare

The Australian challenger bore many names during the summer of 1983. Some of those names flattered, some maligned, but none ridiculed. The list seemed endless, thanks to the ever inventive minds of the huge international press corps gathered in Newport: *Australia II* (the name on Lloyd's International Registry of Ships, and the name emblazoned on her transom); *KA-6*, her sail number; *Roo Ship* (from the kangaroo which adorned her battle standard); *Wonder from Down Under*; *Down Underdog*; *Fast White Mother*; *Rocketship*.

But one name struck a chord of fear in the heart of every 12-Meter sailor racing for the America's Cup: *Great White*. Those two words were really all that needed to be said about her: that in the water she was a methodical, cold-blooded killer, a kind of great white shark relentless with its prey. The name sent a primitive chill up and down the spines of the American defenders and the challengers from other nations.

But the men who race 12-Meters at the America's Cup level have to be men of valor: Crewing a 12-Meter can be a dangerous pastime. Volatile, unpredictable vessels at the best of times, the boats can lurch with a sudden twist when there is a wind shift. *Australia II* had already maimed a crew member, Scotty McAllister. A crane, masthead high, had fallen like the blade of a blunt guillotine and smashed McAllister's arm between wrist and elbow. And for agonizing seconds no one on board had known of his predicament. The wind had stolen his screams.

As the summer wore on, the white boat's mysterious prowess on the water left other competitors physically and emotionally drained. *Great White* left a long casualty list of Canadians, Italians, French, British and even fellow Australians. And defeat—to the driven men who compete for the America's Cup—is an agonizing pain that never recedes.

The red boat, too, had more than one name in the summer of 1983, but the names were far fewer and far less imaginative than the ones given the white boat. There was the Lloyd's registry entry—*Liberty*, a name as proud and dignified as *Australia II*; there was her sail number, *US 40*; and there was the informal *Ruby*, a nickname arrived at partly by way of a Kenny Rogers' song and partly because of her ruby-red hull. But like *Australia II* or *Great White*, *Liberty* acquired a *nom de guerre*: *Red Dog*.

Whether the inspiration for the label came from Alan Bond and his company of challengers or from an inventive member of the press corps is uncertain. The Australian syndicate did indeed refer to the American boat as *Red Dog* in a deliberate attempt to needle Conner and his crew and cast aspersions on the racing prowess of their 12-Meter. The derisive label was also an important part of the Australians' efforts at psyching themselves up for this all-important battle: *Liberty* must be thought of as a dog, the kind of boat from which they had nothing to fear.

But in fact *Liberty*—without any innovations, armed only with the expertise of her crew—proved herself to be a very tough customer on the race course. And the name *Red Dog* underwent a subtle semantic change. It became synonymous with courage and gritty determination.

The American boat is gaining ground....

Conner must decide and he must decide quickly: left or right. It is a heads/tails, evens/odds decision. For Lady Luck has a part in these races, a not insignificant supporting role. The wind is shifting, gusting in pockets of varying strength: tempestuous, self-governing breezes that may be a hint of imminent change. Correctly divining a shift in the wind may prove a tremendous boon to one crew; to another, unprepared for the change, a windshift is a curse.

Conner chooses left, and be it Lady Luck's helping hand or because he is blessed with a nose for the wind, *Liberty*'s sails trap the strength of a major windshift. *Red Dog* powers forward through the bruising waters of the Sound. But the breeze offers nothing to *Great White*, and the Australian boat begins to falter.

Red Dog gains speed. It is a marvelous, heady sensation. The boat begins to skim over the ocean like a stone skipping across a smooth pond, and his new-found momentum fills the heart of Dennis Conner as the wind has filled his sails. The sensation is momentarily overpowering, like the sudden impact of a powerful intoxicant. The waves no longer batter at *Red Dog*. They part and stand aside like spectators giving way to a torch-bearing Olympic runner; they slap at the hull in encouraging applause. Conner savors the moment.

Boat speed is a magic elixir to a man like Conner. Just moments ago the python of defeat was coiling around his neck—and now he has been given another chance. The gap narrows ... eighty feet ... seventy ... sixty ... fifty ... a

Sail Numbers

mere boat length. The red boat seems ready to spear the white, her sword-like bow poised for the fatal thrust.

Conner's concentration is absolute. Directly in front of him is the orange pylon that signals the end of the first leg of the race. With ruthless efficiency, he times his moment. The white boat is closer now: The duel is a slow-motion ballet, exquisite and agonizing. Conner's plan is simplicity itself, but it allows no margin for error. With his greater speed he will tack, turning his boat into the path of *Great White*. If his feeling for time and distance is exactly right, he will slip in just ahead of his opponent's bow, putting *Red Dog* between *Great White* and the pylon. Such a maneuver will accomplish two goals: Conner will be perfectly positioned to round the pylon, and *Australia II* will fall into his windshadow, the disturbed flow of air left by his boat's sails. But if Conner misjudges this maneuver, the result will be catastrophic. Technically the white boat has right-of-way. If Conner errs by as little as a heartbeat, he will either be forced to abandon everything in a desperate effort to avoid the onrushing *Australia II* or the two hulls will collide and Conner will lose the America's Cup in the most ignominious way possible: default by foul.

On board *Fox Hunter II* and *Black Swan*, the tension is electric. It dries lips, beads foreheads, pushes pulse rates to danger zones. Both the Australians and the yachtsmen of the America's Cup committee can read Conner's mind. They know he is about to attempt one of the most dangerous, technically difficult maneuvers in the repertoire of yacht racing.

And suddenly Conner makes his move. *Red*

Dog is on to *Great White*, and before the mind can register what is happening, while it is still only an image before the eye, the red boat is past the white, in front. Conner has pulled it off, his execution flawless. Every horn in the spectator fleet sounds with a furious energy, every whistle is pulled in triumph. The sound rises in an enormous but invisible mountain, a volcanic island erupting from the ocean with a shattering roar. The shock wave rolls inland, washes on to the shorebound spectators and rattles the windowpanes of seaside Newport cottages.

Red Dog wheels around the marker. Stopwatches are started. In metronomic ticks, second hands measure the swift—but not swift enough—progress of *Great White*: ten seconds . . . a boat length . . . twenty seconds . . . two boat lengths . . . twenty-five, twenty-six, twenty-seven, twenty-eight, twenty-nine seconds—stop. The Australian boat rounds the marker twenty-nine seconds, three boat lengths, behind the defender.

Round one is over. *Red Dog* is the early victor.

1:55 pm

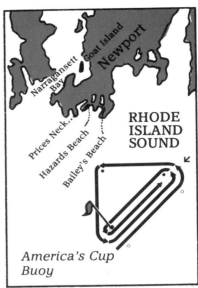

Narragansett Bay

Goat Island

Newport

Prices Neck

Hazards Beach

Bailey's Beach

**RHODE
ISLAND
SOUND**

*America's Cup
Buoy*

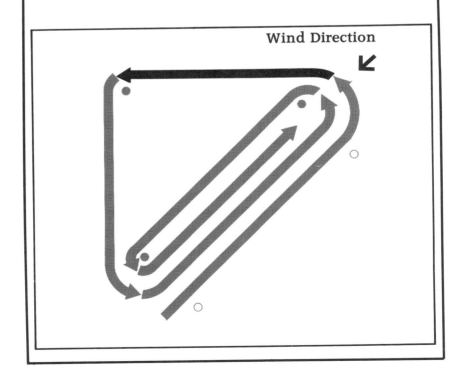

Wind Direction

The Second Leg

Ideals are like stars; you will not succeed in touching them with your hand. But like the seafaring man on the desert of waters, you choose them as your guides, and following them you will reach your destiny.

Carl Schurz

At the helm of *Red Dog*, despite his twenty-nine second lead, Dennis Conner's mood is one of disquiet. He has accomplished his short-term objective: to lead *Great White* after the first weather leg. But he had hoped for a more substantial lead, on the order of a minute, or five to six boat lengths. He has achieved only half that.

As his boat rounded the first mark, he had half turned to watch the other over his shoulder and mentally timed the Australians' sail change: eight seconds flat, a superb set—superior, he grimly noted, to *Red Dog*'s. The Australians' spinnaker, a mammoth, parachute-shaped sail, had filled the instant it was hit by the windstream. For a moment, the hull of *Great White* was lost in a wave trough. It was all sail, a giant, mushrooming cloud rolling omnipotently over the ocean swells, a thing of impossible beauty yet deadly purpose. Now it cast its massive, predatory shadow over Dennis Conner and *Red Dog*.

You have deeply ventured,
But all must do so who would greatly win.   *Byron*

When *Great White*, towed by her tender *Black Swan*, had left her dockside lair at Newport Offshore that day, she did so to the sound of her battle hymn—a popular song by the hard-driving Australian rock band, Men at Work: *Do you come from a land Down Under, / Where women glow and men plunder? / Can't you hear, can't you hear the thunder? / You better run, you better take cover.*

A throng of well-wishers cheered and waved tiny Australian flags and the by-now-familiar Roo flag, as it was dubbed.

On board *Great White*, the flag was run up the forestay, where it snapped aggressively in the freshening sea breeze. It featured a giant, gold kangaroo wearing scarlet boxing gloves. The pugilist kangaroo was set against a field of Australian green. The flag was at once ridiculous and, in the fashion of another great pugilist, Muhammed Ali ("float like a butterfly, sting like a bee"), insolent and taunting.

The flag was not the product of a quirky, adolescent mind. It had been designed by a professional graphic artist, its sole purpose to burrow under the skin of the Americans. The idea was conceived by Warren Jones, the Australian syndicate manager. Other Australian challengers had featured a kangaroo image, but they had all been cut from the same inoffensive cloth: They

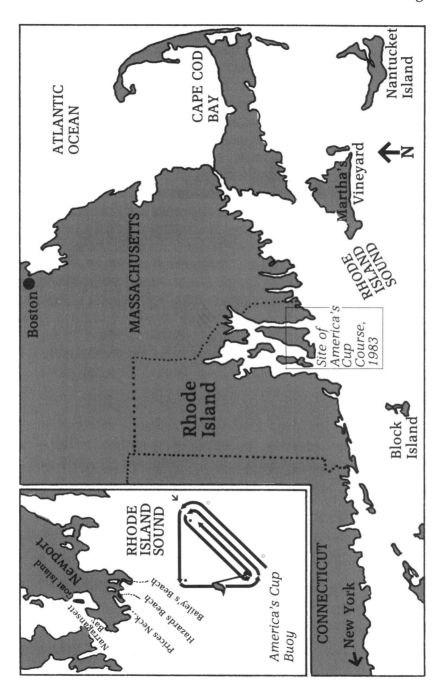

looked like huggable stuffed toys. The 1983 kangaroo was a rough-and-ready customer spoiling for a fight. As the flag snapped in the wind, it snapped in the face of *Red Dog* and particularly in the face of Dennis Conner. It was a thrown-down gauntlet that could not be ignored. Loud and clear it proclaimed that Conner and *Red Dog* could be taken—by *Great White*.

John Bertrand, helmsman of the Australian boat, is a tall, rangy, soft-spoken sailmaker from a bedroom community near Melbourne. Perched on the east coast of Australia a few hundred miles south of Sydney, Melbourne is perhaps the most "English" of Australia's cities, not founded by recalcitrant convicts and their overseers but by "honest" settlers. Australians have a saying that when a stranger arrives in Sydney he is first asked how much money he has, but on arrival in

Roo Flag

Melbourne he is asked what school he attended. The epigram recalls Mark Twain's famous quip: "In Boston they ask, How much does he know? In New York, How much is he worth?" The Sydney/New York, Melbourne/Boston parallel holds true in another way: Sydney has all the hurly-burly of the Big Apple, Melbourne, the staid establishment veneer of Boston. And John Bertrand's personality reflects Melbourne. Although his upbringing is strictly middle class he is, in mannerisms and speech, the perfect gentleman: polite, considerate, unassuming, as polished as an ambassador in observing the protocol and etiquette attendant at Newport during an America's Cup summer.

On this historic morning, as on the other mornings when preparing to do battle with Dennis Conner, his demeanor was deceptively placid. Beneath the outward calm, however, his heart was pumping furiously. Bertrand was acutely aware that he was on the threshold of a kind of immortality.

Most crew members headed below decks as *Australia II* was towed out of Newport Harbor, by Fort Adams, past the foreshore of Castle Hill and the shoreline sloping down to Hammersmith Farm (where in another epoch—although only twenty-five years before—Jacqueline Bouvier and John F. Kennedy had married) and into the east passage of Narragansett Bay, which leads to Rhode Island Sound. The tow was a long one. The crew had been up since dawn and, following a carefully established routine, had breakfasted together at Founders' Hall, the Australian syndicate headquarters in Newport. Some crew members had partaken heartily of the food offered. Others had merely nibbled at their toast. The ride out to the Cup course was a choppy one, and even these veteran sailors were subject to *mal de mer*. But there was another reason for lighter appetites than usual: The upcoming conflict was the deciding race for the trophy that most had spent the better part of three years pursuing. Although to a less grandiose degree than Bertrand, these men, whether grinder, mastman or bowman, felt they were on the threshold of their own immortality.

Once below deck, most curled up on folded sails to snatch some sleep if possible. During the earlier part of the summer, when the consequences had not been so obviously crucial, the movement of the boat, the rhythmic slap of waves against the hull and the keening sound of wind in the naked rigging had been soporific. Sleep had come without effort, despite queasy stomachs and mild pangs of anxiety about races ahead. But on the morning of the seventh race, sleep did not come easily, and the rocking of the boat and the lullaby of wind and waves were far from soothing. Most of the crew tossed and turned on their beds of sailcloth, dozing fitfully if at all.

John Bertrand, regardless of the significance of the race, rarely went below for a catnap. This day, as on others, he stayed at the helm of *Great White*, an island unto himself, immersed in the psychological build-up necessary to prepare himself for the upcoming confrontation with *Red Dog*. Bertrand's mind, like Dennis Conner's, was on destiny.

In his thought patterns, his self-assessment and his view of the outside world, John Bertrand is pragmatic on one hand, mystical and romantic on the other. That dichotomy· was never more apparent than when his mind turned to the America's Cup. The pragmatist in him was certain that his fascination with the Cup was a natural consequence of his passion for yacht racing and for winning. Bertrand could not deny that he was possessed of a deep-seated hatred of losing; he knew he was born to compete, just like a matador trained from childhood for the ring. And according to his wife Rasa,

Bertrand was obsessed with the Cup; if he did not win the "damn thing," it would haunt him forever. The mystical side of his character Bertrand certainly owed to Bant and Nan Cull, his maternal grandparents who, along with Rasa, were his dominant influences.

Bertrand's grandfather had earned his livelihood as a fisherman on Port Phillip Bay, a virtually land-locked body of water south of Melbourne on the Pacific Ocean. Bant Cull always maintained that his grandson had been born with the sea in his blood. But it was Bertrand's grandmother, a remarkable woman (though in her eighties, she remained an active president of her yacht club ladies' committee until her death just weeks before Bertrand's fateful encounter with the Americans), who had introduced him to mystical beliefs about the world and about himself. She always believed that her "Johnny" would win the Cup. There was no logic to this conviction that John Bertrand was now within a race of consecrating—just an other-worldly instinct.

Nan Cull was steeped in the lore and legend of the Cup. Her grandfather, Bertrand's great-great-grandfather, was Tom Pearkes. He had worked for the legendary Sir Thomas Lipton on the construction of Lipton's great racing yachts, all of which bore the name *Shamrock*. Lipton challenged for the Cup five times—and five times he was denied entrance at the door to glory. In 1930, weary and frail of body but still possessed of a lion's heart, he had challenged for the last time with *Shamrock V*. He lost to Harold "Mike" Vanderbilt's *Enterprise*. The Tea King was inconsolable, muttering in his Scottish brogue: "I canna win; I canna win."

Lipton had been an enormously popular man in America. Perhaps it was because, although fabulously wealthy, he had risen from humble origins and had no affectation or arrogance. He had even sojourned for a time in America as a young man, working as a greengrocer's clerk before returning to Scotland to start his own remarkably successful grocery chain. But he never lost the common touch, and his rags-to-riches story was a fairy tale for Depression-era America. Lipton's infatuation with the America's Cup—the rich man's trophy—was part of the magic of that fairy tale. At his final loss, there was reportedly not a dry eye in any speakeasy from Chicago to New York. Even Vanderbilt (a man whom much of America despised because his wealth was inherited) was distraught in victory: "Our hour of triumph, our hour of victory, is all but at hand," he wrote at the finish of the last race and later recorded in his book about the match, "but it is so tempered with sadness that it is almost hollow. To win the America's Cup is glory enough for any yachtsman, but why should we be verging on the disconsolate?"

The young John Bertrand had listened closely to his grandmother's tales of Tom Pearkes, the *Shamrock*s and the wonderfully popular Tea King. Bertrand would follow in Lipton's footsteps, but he would not be a loser. It was his destiny to do what Thomas Lipton and countless others before and after had failed to do: win the Cup.

Below deck in the sail compartment of Bertrand's *Great White*, sunlight flooded through hatch openings in bright oblong patches of color, warming the interior of the boat. It made the crew drowsy, but still sleep would not come. There was no conversation. Idle chit-chat seemed out of place, superficial. Nor was there any of the usual kibitzing, the rough-house humor in which the crew indulged if they were in a playful mood. This day there was only contemplative silence.

On the deck above, the morning air, stirred by the sea breeze, was chill and refreshing. A few hundred yards away, Bertrand could see *Challenge 12*, the trial horse for *Australia II*. At the wheel, he could see the upright profile of Sir James Hardy—the man who had selflessly stepped down, in 1980, from his position as helmsman of *Australia*, permitting Bertrand's promotion.

Thoughts of Hardy's selflessness led Bertrand to contemplate his own crew. They were ten good men, tried and true. He loved each one of them as a brother—and would trust his life to any of them. They represented a curious cross-section of personalities and backgrounds. One was a mathematics teacher, another an army

John Bertrand

officer, another a lawyer, yet another the head of Sobstad Sails in Sydney. Their nicknames—Mad Dog, Ya, Hughey, the Major, Skippy, Scoop, Beasho, Chink and Splash—sounded more like the roll call of a ship that flew the skull and crossbones than of one carrying the battle standard of a proud nation, the gold kangaroo with the scarlet boxing gloves.

It struck Bertrand, though, that his crew was rather like a band of pirates. Just as the sailor-robbers of an earlier age had coveted stolen gold and treasure, so the crew of *Great White* lusted after another, but equally precious, plunder: one hundred and thirty-four ounces of silver—the America's Cup.

Great White casts a predatory shadow . . . .

The wind is behind and abeam of the boats during the second leg, the first power reach. Only on this leg has *Red Dog* previously established herself as clearly superior to *Great White*. Only once on the second leg have the Australians outpaced the Americans; that was in race one and by the slightest of margins—a mere two seconds. On this power reach over the next three races, *Red Dog* gained an average of seventeen seconds on *Great White*. Yet unaccountably, during races five and six, the Australians improved their performance. They shaved the Americans' superiority on the first power reach to a single second. Conner must return *Red Dog* to her earlier mastery on this leg if he is to hold off the Australians' expected downwind charge later in the race.

John Bertrand rounds the first mark gritting his teeth. He knows the Americans re-configured their boat after their loss in the sixth race. Rumor has it *Red Dog* is half a ton of ballast lighter; Bertrand figures it is closer to a ton. The Americans have also added sail area, his trained eye notes. The results are showing. *Red Dog* is definitely more nimble on this bright, cloudless day than in earlier races. But this only strengthens Bertrand's determination. For despite all the hype and theatrics surrounding the America's Cup, there is no denying that this is indeed turning into the race of the century.

He tests the mood on his boat. The tension is stretched as tight as a drumskin. He has to lessen that tension, and it is a delicate task—rather like defusing a time bomb. A slip of the tongue, a frown, a misplaced gesture can sow the seeds of disaster. The ten men in his crew make up an infantry section; as the eleventh, Bertrand is section leader. With *Great White* under fire, one slip-up, one error in judgment can cost him his section—and Australia's chance to wrest the America's Cup from the world's most powerful nation. Bertrand must exude absolute confidence in himself and in his men. He wills himself to be calm. He will not break under the enormous strain of months of grueling combat.

He calls to mind one of modern history's great players, and one of his heroes, warrior-statesman Winston Churchill. The year was 1941, the month October. The infamy of Pearl Harbor and America's declaration of war lay six weeks in the future, and Hitler's shadow loomed large. Churchill and the British Commonwealth stood with their backs to the wall. Churchill had been invited to deliver a speech at Harrow, his alma mater. His famous declaration—"Never give in, never give in, never, never, never"—has become Bertrand's own motto of courage and honor. Silently he wills this motto into the heart and soul of every man on board the white boat. And by some alchemy, it works. He senses the tension dissipating, its poisonous fumes drifting harmlessly away.

That is just as well, because a shift in wind brings a new threat, filling the sails of *Red Dog* and denying Bertrand's boat life-giving strength. Bertrand's navigator, Grant Simmer, delivers an unsettling report: *Liberty* is increasing her lead.

In his cockpit Dennis Conner hears Halsey Herreshoff, his navigator, announce that *Red Dog* is clawing, yard by hard-fought yard, away from *Great White*. Like individual grains of sand in an hourglass, every fraction of a foot is precious to the American boat. The fierceness of the competition has been confirmed in every race—but none more so than in race four. That race was sailed on a glorious day of sunshine and hazy azure skies. *Red Dog* found the splendor of the day to her liking; she won the race. But her winning margin was a razor-thin forty-three seconds. More disturbing to the Americans, however, were the results of a leg-by-leg post-mortem. Over three legs (the second, third and fourth—two power reaches, one weather reach), *Liberty* had not gained a single yard, not a single second. *Australia II* tenaciously hung on, refusing to give an inch over twelve miles of treacherous, shifting wind and wave-tossed ocean.

The New York Yacht Club, the yachting world (including its Australian members) and the press were unanimous for once when it came to that race: Conner's performance had been nothing short of brilliant. His start had been daring. He had crossed the white boat's bow by inches in a hair-raising maneuver called a port-tack. The Australian boat had the right-of-way. It was tantamount to a car swinging directly across the path of oncoming traffic just as the signal light turns green. Bertrand had been dumbfounded by Conner's audacity, having expected *Red Dog* to pass to his stern. Yet Conner had managed to win by little more than half a minute; despite their three-to-one series lead, the Americans could not afford to be complacent.

Dennis Conner

He had momentarily checked *Australia II's* momentum with a win in race four, but brooding in the background like black storm clouds was a nagging question. Conner would have to repeat that perfect race if he was to win the Cup.

It is fatal to enter any war without the will to win it.
                                                    MacArthur

At approximately the same hour as *Australia II* was being towed to its rendezvous with destiny, *Liberty* was being readied for battle. A towing cable was strung between it and the fifty-three-foot Hatteras *Fire Three*, the American tender. *Red Dog*'s lair was at the Williams & Manchester shipyard on Lee's Wharf. The wharf is perhaps two or three hundred yards from Newport Offshore, home of *Great White*. It was possible to hear faintly the pounding Australian battle hymn drifting over the waterfront in fitful bursts: *Down Under . . . men plunder . . . hear the thunder . . . run . . . take cover.*

It was not music meant to soothe the savage breast of *Red Dog. Fire Three* responded with the American battle anthems—*Chariots of Fire* and the theme from *The Empire Strikes Back*—with amplifiers turned up to deafening decibel levels, effectively drowning out Men at Work, although at the risk of eardrum damage to those American supporters dockside of *Red Dog.*

It was a moment of stirring inspiration for the American yachtsmen, sea-warriors about to fight a dreaded foe under the colors of their nation's flag. And that was exactly what Dennis Conner and his crew felt they were. In the fratricidal bloodbath that was the American defense elimination series, *Liberty* had lacked charisma. She had backed unexpectedly into the match against the Australians, having defeated one of the most historied boats ever to defend the Cup, *Courageous* (a yacht that oozed charisma like her one-time skipper, the flamboyant media czar Ted Turner), and *Defender*—a slow boat, to be sure, but with her royal blue hull, one of the sleekest and most beautiful yachts ever to grace America's Cup waters. (*Defender* was considered by many to be the most elegant boat in Newport during the summer of 1983—a crown she stole from the Italian entry, *Azzurra*, named for the azure water and crystalline sky of her Mediterranean home at Costa Smeralda on the island of Sardinia.)

Not only was *Liberty* seen as something of a thorn between two American roses, it was forced into the role of ugly step-sister, an unwilling foil to the Cinderella of the summer, *Australia II*. It also had an apparently mean-spirited mentor in the form of the New York Yacht Club, whose high-handed, imperialist manners frayed the good nature of just about everybody in Newport. Conner and his boat suffered by association.

Yet now that the chips were down, now that *Red Dog* was up against it, American fans had, as Dennis Conner predicted they would, rallied to the cause of their champion. His crew realized that they were about to begin a battle for the honor of their country. With stirring music ringing in their ears, they found there were lumps in their throats. One spoke for them all: "I felt I could break stone with my bare hands." *Red Dog* would need every ounce of this Herculean resolve to contend with *Great White*'s strength.

Like his adversary, Conner did not retire to the cramped confines below deck for a prerace nap during the eight-mile tow-out to the America's Cup buoy. His mind, like Bertrand's, was dwelling on lofty and disturbing notions of immortality and destiny. Conner had already had a glimpse of eternal fame, of course: In 1980 he had joined the ranks of Stevens, Vanderbilt, Bavier, Cunningham, Mosbacher, Hood, Turner—the pantheon of men who had successfully defended the America's Cup. But now he was in peril of becoming the first American to lose the Cup.

Conner is rarely given to deep philosophical introspection. And his attitude toward destiny is rather more pragmatic than his rival's: Glory is forged only through hard work and determination. It does not descend from on high.

Conner, unlike Bertrand, had no family ties to the America's Cup; he had, in fact, no sea heritage at all. He came out of middle-class San Diego, a city that sprawls in one direction to the edge of the Pacific Ocean and in another to the Mexican-American border. Dust and fly-ridden Tijuana, a favorite hangout for San Diego's teenage population, is a fifteen-minute spin down one of the many freeways lacing southern California. Booze, dope and illicit sex are plentiful and cheap there. Conner, however, turned his back on these sleazy attractions. He went in the other direction: to the cleansing and character-building challenge of the sea. The San Diego Yacht Club became a home away from home for the shy, introverted teenager. Conner could not afford his own boat so he crewed for anyone who offered him a berth. He acquired a permanent deep-water tan and, of more lasting importance, his distinctive brand of self-confidence—not to mention the incalculably valuable experience of sailing all manner of racing yacht.

Conner admits that as a teenager he suffered from an inferiority complex. But for some reason that complex did not inhibit his drive to be a winner. Years later he was to call his autobiography *No Excuse to Lose.* As an apprentice in the world of yacht racing, Dennis Conner adopted a time-honored creed: Practice makes perfect. He modified the creed slightly to read: Practice

Liberty First

and preparation make perfect. This simple formula is the key to understanding Dennis Conner. He out-practiced and out-prepared his opponents. Add to this his unwavering focus on whatever his goal might be—and of course the ultimate goal was the America's Cup—and, as the yacht racing world discovered, Conner was a virtually unbeatable competitor.

But sitting at the helm of *Liberty* as she was towed through the Newport chop, Conner reflected that the American dream could shatter before his eyes on this day of impossible allure, of beneficent sun, sky and wind.

The battle now before Conner on the brilliant, unfeeling waters of Rhode Island Sound had long been more than a sporting contest. It had something to do with the magnitude and glory of the America's Cup tradition but was even more the result of the attitude that Conner and his opponent, John Bertrand, brought to the race. Both men could sense imminent immortality: for one, victory; for the other, inglorious defeat.

Red Dog is clawing, yard by hard-fought yard, away from Great White . . . .

It is shortly before two o'clock in the afternoon. *Red Dog* and *Great White* can see the orange sausage-shaped wing marker that indicates the end of this power reach. Beyond the marker, despite the diligent efforts of the Coast Guard, hundreds of power boats have encroached on the race course. The result is a wind umbrella, pockets of air ricocheting in helter-skelter directions like the demented progress of the ball in a pinball machine. The spectator fleet has formed an artificial reef creating confused, lumpy seas. Sailing conditions are tricky and unstable, the wind is light and patchy.

Both Conner and Bertrand are intimately familiar with the treacherous killing ground of Rhode Island Sound. This is the Australian's fourth America's Cup campaign, and Dennis Conner's second as helmsman. Both men have excelled at trapping less worthy adversaries in just such conditions, leaving those unfortunate souls to gasp and flounder in a windhole like fish out of water. Now they are wary of such entrapments. In both helmsmen every nerve fiber is concentrated on deciphering the wayward wind. Breezes play hide-and-seek on the water. They betray their presence two hundred and three hundred yards in the distance, slivers of quicksilver shimmying across sapphire seas. As the two boats haul up on the marker, the air turns almost mushy, and the sea is in turmoil.

Red Dog hits the marker first, careening between it and an anchored Coast Guard cutter like an ice skater cutting a corner on an inside blade. Stop-watch buttons are immediately depressed. Behind, *Great White* glides to the marker with balletic grace. As she rounds the pylon her parachute-spinnaker is collapsed, and within seconds a smaller green-and-gold canopy is deployed. It blossoms like a tropical flower— abruptly and with intense beauty under the powerful afternoon sun. It lifts the white boat forward in chase after the red, white and blue orchid floating above the American yacht. Stopwatch buttons are hit again. Elapsed time: forty-five seconds. The Americans have gained sixteen seconds.

2:18 pm

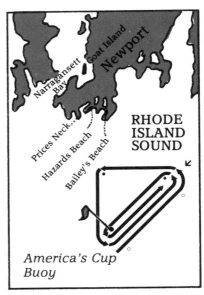

RHODE
ISLAND
SOUND

*America's Cup
Buoy*

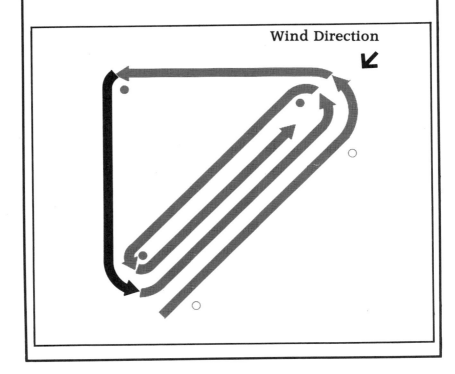

Wind Direction

The Third Leg

Their ships are swift as a bird or a thought.

Homer

John Bertrand looks down at the steering wheel. His knuckles are ivory white. He is gripping the wheel, a man possessed. Possessed by what? Fear. Panic. Desperation. Indecision. *Defeat*. He ought not even to form or think the word, let alone give it voice. But suddenly the specter of defeat hovers, staring him in the face, dissolving his defense mechanisms. Bertrand is at the breaking point. It is a point he must confront, a rite of passage, for it is now that the real John Bertrand will emerge. In an eerie way his life to date has been a series of way stations delivering him up to this moment of truth. But what surprises and unsettles him is the lack of warning. He had expected to be able to prepare, to be able, like a Biblical warrior, to gird himself for battle.

Suddenly John Bertrand—a Lear on the high seas—wants to shriek at the top of his lungs. *Fuck you! You goddamn son-of-a-bitch! Fuck you!* The words remain within, but Bertrand finds his voice: *We are going to nail these bastards!*

Bertrand's fury has a profound effect, not only on his own psyche but on that of his crew. He has transformed the insidious premonition of defeat into a new defiance, and the target is the hated *Red Dog*. To a man the crew raise and turn their heads in Bertrand's direction. Bertrand, despite his calm exterior, is actually possessed of a mercurial temperament. His crew have previously been exposed to outbursts of temper. But instinctively they take this outburst for what it is—raised-fist defiance. And to a man on *Australia II*, sagging spirits and hope are revived. *Great White*'s killer instinct has been resurrected.

Inside, Bertrand is shaking. He is stunned by the primitive savagery of his emotions. The pressure of this race, the intensity of the competition, has gone beyond rational comprehension. Only Bertrand knows how close *Great White* has come to collapsing under the pressure, and that his outburst has been triggered by the phantom of defeat—not by the vision of attainable victory.

A grievous burden was thy birth to me;
Tetchy and wayward was thy infancy.

Shakespeare

Yacht designers and midwives have common ground: They are frequently confronted with deliveries—boats on the one hand, babies on the other—that are remarkable for their protracted and complicated birthing labor. Midwives will also confide a cruel truth: Mother Nature is not perfect. All who enter this world do not come with ten toes and ten fingers. The intricacies of a 12-Meter yacht are, on a technological plane, as comparatively complicated as the anatomy of the human body. Designers of 12-Meter yachts will reluctantly admit that they, like Mother Nature, are not perfect. All 12-Meters do not come into this world endowed with the perfect keel and hull configuration. Indeed, the rare exception makes stark proof of that reality.

The birth of the boat that was to defend in the twenty-fifth America's Cup challenge was the most difficult and bloody labor in Cup history. To complicate matters it was a multiple birth; it had become common for major syndicates to produce two or more boats, each with design variations. Party to this fertile process for the 1983 defense were the New York Yacht Club's America's Cup committee, the Madison Avenue firm of Sparkman & Stephens (patriarch of American yacht design firms), Johan Valentijn, who would design the red-hulled *Liberty*, and Dennis Conner, its helmsman and skipper. As possible contenders were born, paternity became an issue: Who had fathered which?

As serious defects appeared in each boat, the designers, the helmsmen and other mortals swept up in the drama of the America's Cup defense began playing God. If their progeny displayed the slightest imperfection—and the summer of 1983 was rife with imperfection, both in men and in boats—out came (without a touch of remorse) the cutting and welding torches. Surgery was the order of the day; Newport Offshore, the shipyard responsible for the construction of *Liberty*, became a nautical operating theater. As the frequency of surgery increased, jokes began to make the rounds. The operations were called tummy or butt tucks depending on where the acetylene torch was applied. It was not, however, mere cosmetic snipping and clipping that the designers and shipwrights were about; it was major reconstructive surgery. Yachts were matter-of-factly dismembered, then welded back together and thrown out on the ocean. There, the test was simple enough— sink or swim.

Unfortunately some of the hopefuls that had been designed and built at great cost and with such loving care—notably *Magic* and *Spirit of America*—seemed more inclined to do the former. They were called dogs, but with their weld scars and jagged, soldered seams, they might have been aquatic incarnations of Frankenstein's monster.

And so it went: an exhausting schedule of cutting, fixing, rearranging and putting back together again. The blue flame of acetylene burned late into the black Newport night, searching for the elusive lines of which perfection is made. But it was not to be. The Almighty, whose nationalistic leanings would be questioned time and again as the summer unfolded, might be forgiven a knowing smile.

The design history of America's Cup defenders is long and distinguished—two centuries bridged by an unbroken bloodline of American genius. Yet, the number of designers belonging to this elite fraternal group are few: Nathanael Herreshoff, Edward Burgess, his son W. Starling Burgess, Olin Stephens and, more recently, Bill Langen.

Starling Burgess had collaborated with Stephens, then a twenty-eight-year-old *wunderkind*, in the creation of the legendary *Ranger*. In the summer of 1937, *Ranger* won thirty-two out of thirty-four races and, skippered by the illustrious Harold "Mike" Vanderbilt, beat the British challenger *Endeavour II* four races to none. In the second race of that year's final, which was run over a thirty-mile equilateral triangle, the American yacht beat the English boat by eighteen minutes, an astounding margin of victory. In yachting terms, it was equivalent to a miler lapping an opponent.

Olin Stephens went on to design some of the truly great racing yachts of that era and this. The 12-Meter rule (a measurement based on a formula taking into account water line length, sail area, displacement and girth measurement) now associated with the Cup has been in effect for more than eighty years of America's Cup racing. Yet before the summer of 1983 only one yacht, Olin Stephens' *Intrepid* (1967), had been called truly revolutionary.

Other boats with new design features culminating in *Freedom*, the successful defender of 1980, had been

Johan Valentijn

described as evolutionary rather than revolutionary. But in the summer of 1983, the notorious *Australia II* staked a strong claim to challenging *Intrepid*'s reputation.

Olin Stephens, on the eve of becoming an octogenarian, is one of the quintessential gentlemen of the American yachting scene. By 1983 he had turned over much of the day-to-day running of Sparkman & Stephens' 12-Meter operations to his gifted young protégé, Bill Langen. Nevertheless, he kept his hand in the business of designing 12-Meters slotted to defend the America's Cup. He was naturally disappointed with the performance of *Spirit of America*. He must also have been more than a little shocked at the cavalier manner in which the racing thoroughbreds he had worked on for half a century were being treated in the early 1980s. Traditionally there was an integrity, a wholeness and a harmony to racing-yacht design. Tune-ups were certainly commonplace, but such wholesale reconstruction as was happening in Newport seemed almost a violation of the spirit of the sport.

The concerns of Stephens and other traditionalists notwithstanding, one thing was certain in the creation of the 1983 American 12-Meters: Winning was the only game in town.

Enter Dennis Conner, the catalyst in the drive for the ultimate 12-Meter. Conner issued Bill Langen and Johan Valentijn a simple ultimatum: Build a faster *Freedom*. Both designers having failed to deliver on that concisely stated objective (with Valentijn's *Magic* ending up as a Newport tourist attraction while Langen's *Spirit of America* was demoted to the role of trial horse), Conner ordered that a third 12-Meter be designed. This was a historic edict: *three* boats for one syndicate! The cost (each boat fully outfitted, including sail inventory, came with a price tag just shy of a million dollars) sent shock waves rippling through yacht clubs across America.

The scheme of Conner and syndicate chief Ed du Moulin called for a collaboration between Valentijn and Sparkman & Stephens, or, more specifically, between the Netherlands-born designer (now a naturalized U.S. citizen) and Bill Langen. Such a collaboration was not unprecedented—Valentijn and Ben Lexcen, designer of *Great White*, had jointly delivered the 1977 and 1980 challenger *Australia*. Nor was it anticipated that Valentijn and Langen would experience difficulty working together. After all, the Dutchman had spent five years of apprenticeship with Sparkman & Stephens, working directly under Olin Stephens. Yet for reasons that have never surfaced from the muddy waters of speculation (the most common story is that neither designer would share the secrets of his craft with the other), Langen and Valentijn were unable to arrive at a meeting of their creative minds.

Re-enter Dennis Conner with yet another Napoleonic edict: The third boat, which would be *Liberty*, would be designed not by the *éminence grise* of American yacht designers, Olin Stephens, but by a relative newcomer, Johan Valentijn. Pupil had deposed professor, and the American yachting establishment was flabbergasted. Olin Stephens was too much of a gentleman to go public with his thoughts on this most shocking and manifestly unjust decision. But the disappointment, the fact that he had been damned with faint praise—everyone acknowledged his brilliance, his unrivalled contribution to countless Cup campaigns, but in the same breath it was still "thanks but no thanks"—must have placed a heavy burden on his heart, a heart already saddened by the lackluster performance of *Spirit of America*.

Johan Valentijn tried to put the tempest behind him. He dutifully sat down at the drafting board in his Newport office—it was hotly whispered that Dennis Conner, who is neither a naval architect nor an engineer, stood over his shoulder the entire time—and went to work on the lines of *Liberty*. What emerged was a conventional 12-Meter, a boat with a long water line and a light displacement (in fact, the lightest 12-Meter ever built), a boat designed to be at home in the light winds and sloppy seas of Rhode Island Sound.

Beauty like hers is genius.

Dante Gabriel Rossetti

If *Liberty* was born of refined American know-how, the Australian challenger seemed to spring like an incubus from a distant cauldron.

She was constructed in great secrecy in Steve Ward's shipyard in Perth. Only a handful of men were permitted to witness her birth: the boat builders, the inner council of the *Australia II* syndicate (Alan Bond, owner; Warren Jones, syndicate chief executive officer; Tom Schnackenberg, sailmaker and, of course, her helmsman, John Bertrand). As the sixty-five-foot-long boat took shape, security tightened. Entrance to the inner sanctum was rigorously monitored. And even within the inner sanctum, a holy-of-holies existed. A large tarpaulin enclosed *Great White*'s massive underbelly. Within the shroud was the Australian boat's secret design feature, her keel.

News of this unprecedented security gradually made its way as far as Newport. What was going on inside that shipyard? Behind its tall cyclone fence, it was rumored, there were laser beams and other sophisticated electronic alarms. Only machine-gun toting sentries, spotlights and vicious guard dogs were needed to complete the picture of a maximum-security stalag.

And if the shipyard looked a little like a fortress, the inner sanctum was like the Vatican, and the tarpaulin tent the Sistine Chapel. In this chapel, a nautical Michelangelo was at work. Or perhaps more accurately a Leonardo da Vinci, a genius who was both engineer and artist; for *Australia II* was the progeny of both art and science.

The man who created *Australia II* was Ben Lexcen. Lexcen has proven himself to be without peer (perhaps with the exception of Olin Stephens) in the design of ocean racing yachts—of which the 12-Meter is considered the *ne plus ultra*. And yet this is a man with little formal education. He started school late, at the age of ten, and he left to find his way in the world at the ripe old age of fourteen.

Ben Lexcen

Lexcen's life has been shaped by the Great Outback and the sea, the twin foundations upon which the Australian character is built. He was born in Boggabri, a small, unimposing town in a majestic outback area of deeply cut gorges and inviting forests. In the Outback, the sun can shine day after day for years, and brushfires can be sparked and spread so swiftly that the landscape is transformed from paradise into a vast, raging inferno, to end up charred, blackened and utterly desolate. It is, brushfire aside, a land that has, according to D.H. Lawrence, "subtle, remote, formless beauty, more poignant than anything ever experienced before." It is the land of Ayers Rock, that huge, mystical, instantly recognizable landmark in the middle of the red, sun-baked desert. The Outback lures the wanderer with its phantasmagoric beauty; but that same wanderer runs the very genuine risk of death beneath the pitiless sun. In the Great Outback, water or other succour is rarely there when needed.

When Lexcen was still a child, his family moved to the seacoast, following in the footsteps of countless Australians before them. Arnold Toynbee has said that Australian cities lie basking on the country's beaches like whales that have taken to the land again. In fact, Australian settlements come not like whales from the sea but rather like hapless birds driven from the immense, uninhabitable interior to cling to seaside sanctuaries. The world's least densely populated country, Australia is also the most highly urbanized. And more than ninety percent of all Australians live within walking distance of water. By the sea at Newcastle, north of Sydney, Lexcen developed a deep and abiding passion for sailing. In this, too, he is typically Australian.

Lexcen became a world-class sailor. In his youth, he won the world championship in the class for the Flying Dutchman, a high-performance boat that requires not only an instinct for the sea and wind but also the strength and hand-eye coordination of a natural athlete. Now in middle age, Lexcen does not give the impression of being gifted with any particular athletic grace or agility. He is a big bear of a man with a shambling gait, an avuncular warmth and charm and a *bon mot* wit as dry and delicious as a well-mixed martini. There is something of the absent-minded professor about him; behind the silver-rimmed spectacles, one often suspects, is a mind off in the clouds, regardless of the issue or idea at hand. It is an endearing but vexatious quality to those who depend on his genius—to John Bertrand and his crew, for instance.

In his twenties, Ben Lexcen turned his free-wheeling imagination to yacht design. In the tradition of *America*'s creator, George Steers, and other great racing yacht designers, Lexcen's is a mind unfettered by convention. Bob Bavier, a greatly respected American yachtsman linked for almost fifty years with America's defense of the Cup (skipper of *Constellation*, the 1964 Cup defender), had stated as recently as 1980 that the chance of a breakthrough in 12-Meter design was "remote, if not nonexistent." But with *Australia II*, Lexcen would prove that the remote, indeed the nonexistent, did exist.

Lexcen had previously designed a number of worthy yachts: *Mercedes III*, *Apollo*, *Gingko*. Each had been a winner of a prestigious international yachting event: the Admiralty's Cup (ocean yacht racing's pre-eminent team event); the Fastnet Race; the Sydney to Hobart; the Newport to Bermuda. His name was greatly respected. But he had designed some truly dreadful boats as well. The failures were described by his fellow Aussies as "Bennyurisms." *Apollo III*, a fifty-footer, was a failure of epic proportions. But Lexcen's weakness could also be his strength. He took chances, pushed himself beyond the bounds of the orthodox. The tried and true simply did not exist for him. He gave his mind full rein—and wherever it took him on the drafting board, the blueprint for a boat was born. If a concept was too off-beat, too unorthodox, it might fail—but fail heroically.

He had also designed 12-Meters before: *Australia*, in collaboration with Johan Valentijn, which had lost to *Freedom* in the 1980 America's Cup , and *Courageous* in 1977. He had designed *Southern Cross* as the 1974 Australian challenger (loser also to *Courageous*). His 12-Meters had been fast, but they had not been design breakthroughs. The American 12-Meters remained in a class unto themselves thanks to Olin Stephens, Lexcen's nemesis.

Thus, when the rumors started circulating about a new design feature on *Australia II*, the yacht racing world was not taken aback. Ben Lexcen was a gambler, at times possessed of amazing clairvoyance, at other times . . . well, even his flops were never less than good conversation pieces. With the approach of the 1983 America's Cup summer, the entire 12-Meter world—from the New York Yacht Club to Marblehead in Massachusetts to Cowes on the Isle of Wight—kept a slightly jaundiced but, nevertheless, watchful eye on Ben Lexcen's latest creation.

The America's Cup defender is chosen by a less formal and far more subjective series of elimination rounds than are used in the selection of the challenger. The challenge elimination series comprises three round-robin contests, at the conclusion of which the top four foreign yachts are paired as semi-finalists. The two yachts emerging victorious from the semi-finals then meet in a best four-out-of-seven match to decide which will challenge for the America's Cup. The New York Yacht Club America's Cup committee schedules three trials—preliminary, observation and final—in its search for the right yacht and the right helmsman. For well over a century this system has proven successful. The proposition is basic: put the yachts head-to-head on the killing ground (the waters off Newport) and let them battle it out. It is essentially a Darwinian system: The fittest will survive. The trial system breeds match-hard yachts and match-hard helmsmen. It is, however, a system rife with Machiavellian intrigue. In America, even within the supposed Corinthian realm of yacht racing, politics are never far from the surface.

But politics and intrigue aside, the New York Yacht Club has never wanted for yachts vying for the opportunity and honor of defending the Cup and American glory. In fact, so intense has been this competition over the years that often the America's Cup matches themselves have been anticlimactic, the conclusion foregone in favor of the American defender.

The summer of 1983 (after the early demise of *Magic* and *Spirit of America*) saw three boats represented by two syndicates go head-to-head for the right to defend the Cup: They were *Liberty*, *Defender* and *Courageous*.

Defender and *Courageous* were stablemates. Their syndicate, far distant from the bastions of the New York Yacht Club, was funded by diverse sources: the People-to-People Sports Committee, a sports funding group formed during the Eisenhower presidency; Leonard Greene, owner of *Courageous* and holder of the patents on a number of lucrative aircraft instrument systems; Nick and Jane Heyl (Nick is manager of the Kingston Trio, while Jane's uncle is Tom Watson of the IBM fortune); and two eminently wealthy Texas oilmen, O.L. Pitts and Lee Smith. There were also contributions from a number of friends and supporters not as affluent as the aforementioned but nevertheless interested in giving Dennis Conner and the red boat a run for their money. The *Defender/Courageous* syndicate would need every donation. Its monthly Newport bill exceeded two hundred thousand dollars.

The American preliminary round got under way on June 18th, the same day the first foreign challenge round-robin series was started. It was a typically foggy New England morning. By the time the sun had burned away the sea mist, it was readily apparent that the summer of 1983 would not be a repeat of the summer of 1980. During the earlier summer, *Freedom*, skippered by Dennis Conner, established her clear superiority from the outset. Her final record, forty-seven wins in fifty-two starts, speaks volumes. But in 1983, *Liberty* gave early warnings of displaying no such mastery over *Courageous* and *Defender*. The summer was going to be a long and arduous trial for all three boats but in particular for Dennis Conner and *Red Dog*.

Conner is not a popular hero. Those in American yachting circles either love to hate him—or hate to love him. His offhand yet imperious decision to construct three new boats for the twenty-fifth defense did not endear him to all. Indeed, that decision crystallized a new reality about the America's Cup—that it had left the world of amateur sport to join the ranks of commercial competition. It was now edging toward the tawdry—to the genteel yachting traditionalists, at least—sphere of professional sport. This development, for which many blamed Conner, did not sit well with a great number of American yachtsmen. What had become of the amateur sport ethic? they asked. Their most visible spokesman was Tom Blackaller, helmsman of *Defender*.

Conner and Blackaller are as unlike each other as are Dr. Jekyll and Mr. Hyde. Conner is burly and undistinguished in appearance and a man of few words. The words that are spoken are chosen with parsimonious care. The silver-haired Blackaller, on the other hand, is matinee-idol handsome (a middle-aged Errol Flynn, in the words of one female admirer). He is flamboyant and loquacious, a man of many words—most of them spat out in rapid-fire, machine-gun delivery. He is the kind of man the media love to take to their hearts: garrulous, colorful, quotable.

Blackaller's assessment of Dennis Conner's obsession with winning was as blunt as it was critical. The Californian's take-no-prisoners approach to the America's Cup was overkill. The challengers (read Australians) were not stormtroopers of the Evil Empire and the Americans were not the Defenders of the Faith. As Tom Blackaller would say: It was, goddamnit, a yacht race—not Armageddon.

But when Conner explained and defended his approach, he spoke for the nation as well as for himself: I am representing three hundred million Americans, he would say; they are counting on me to win. He committed himself heart and soul to the achievement of this noble goal. No one for a moment doubted Conner's sincerity. He saw the America's Cup symbolically. It was not simply a trophy to be won or lost. It represented the best in America: ingenuity, resourcefulness, perseverance, a striving for excellence. He, Dennis Conner, was not being unsportsmanlike. He was out to win an international and hugely prestigious event. Americans are winners, not losers. That has been the tradition of America, the tradition of the America's Cup: a trophy wrested originally from the world's best, Britain, almost a century and a half ago. Now America was the world's best and he, Dennis Conner, was the embodiment of the best in America. He had not been born with a silver spoon in his mouth. He had climbed to the summit the American pioneer way, by old-fashioned sweat and toil. Blackaller could be damned—and goddamn (Conner could also be colorful when the occasion demanded) the expense, the endless internecine squabbling, the backbiting and the backstabbing.

Conner, alone in the American camp, knew the seriousness of the threat posed by *Great White*. The Australians, under syndicate owner Alan Bond, were sparing no expense, leaving no stone of design or training unturned. And Conner knew John Bertrand. They had sailed together on the yacht *Williwaw* on a race from Florida to the Bahamas. They had taken turns at the helm; *Williwaw* had won. And each man had got the measure of the other. Dennis Conner knew that John Bertrand was good, too damned good. Conner knew something else about the outwardly placid Australian, that beneath his quiet exterior, like a sharp sword hidden in a handsome scabbard, beat the heart of a match-race killer. Bertrand and the Australians had been to the Newport well on four successive challenges. Each time they had tasted bitter defeat, but each time they went home the wiser. Never before had they mounted such an aggressive, well-organized, thoroughly prepared campaign as in the summer of 1983. The Aussies lusted for American blood. Conner intended to ensure that it would not be his they spilled.

And so Blackaller and Conner sparred on land like two bitter, quarrelsome Medici princes. On the waters of Rhode Island Sound, they were so absorbed in their fratricidal bickering that they forgot about the third boat, *Courageous*, and John Kolius, the third helmsman.

Kolius was the new kid in town. He hailed from

Houston, Texas, and was tall, blue-eyed and blond. He was also unassuming, a Gary Cooper type, quiet and competent—the sort of gunslinger who doesn't broadcast how quick he is on the draw. John Kolius arrived in Newport without fuss or fanfare. He just went about quietly doing his job—trying to unsaddle that winner-take-all hombre Conner and that likeable but hotshot desperado Blackaller. He came within an eyelash of succeeding. In fact, he and *Courageous* did gun down Blackaller and *Defender* on the race course. Against Conner and *Liberty* he did not fare so well. Between August 25th, the last day on which *Defender* raced, and September 2nd, *Liberty* and *Courageous* squared off eight times: Conner won six of those races. On September 2nd, Conner and *Liberty* were officially announced by the New York Yacht Club America's Cup committee as the defenders of the Cup.

Let others probe the mystery if they can.   Roethe

The challenger, *Australia II,* arrived in Newport via container ship after a voyage of twelve thousand miles and several weeks. She had been shipped from Fremantle Harbour on the west coast of Australia, had crossed the Indian Ocean, rounded the Cape of Good Hope at the toe of the African continent and traveled the length and breadth of the South Atlantic, making landfall under the eternally vigilant eyes of the Statue of Liberty. Little more than a stone's throw away, in mid-Manhattan, members of the New York Yacht Club were paying rather less attention.

Once in America, *Australia II* was towed by her tender, *Black Swan,* the hundred-plus miles up the length of Long Island Sound. After a journey of better than a day, she took up residence in her berth at Newport Offshore, opposite Goat Island. There, for the first time, her competitors saw her gleaming white hull with the twin gold-and-green (the Australian colors) racing stripes just below her gunwales and the tiny, demonic kangaroo on the pennant at her bow.

Viewed bow-on, she truly resembled the frightful jaws of a great white shark. Her body, too, was shark-like; she had the clean, swept-back look of a sleekly powerful torpedo. She was painted in a white enamel as pure, and pristine as a wintry alpine meadow. Yet in the summer noon, and surrounded by the glare of the ocean, she was as radiant as glowing Carrara marble.

Great White was a wonder to behold; on that there was unanimous agreement. But then, there are no wallflowers among 12-Meters; they are all spectacular beauties until they hit the uncompromising waters of Rhode Island Sound, where performance, not beauty, will ultimately endear them to the sailing world. What really commanded interest about this yacht was her skirt, the green polyethylene sheet that screened her underhull, her keel.

Ben Lexcen had the keel mold fashioned at workshops in Sydney amid the most stringent secrecy. It had been shipped to Perth and cast in a single gigantic unit by a government foundry. The keel was then transported to Steve Ward's shipyard and there, in the inner sanctum, it was to be welded to the hull of *Australia II*. Painters, planers and sanders labored within the tentlike tarpaulin in appalling conditions. The outside air temperature in the early days of construction soared to one hundred degrees F, with the mercury often hitting one hundred and twenty degrees inside the tarpaulin. Lexcen had deliberately cast the keel to one-eighth of an inch beyond design specifications. That one-eighth inch was planed down and polished by hand until the keel had the satiny luster of platinum.

Rumours about the mystery keel had been making the rounds for months, since construction on the boat had begun. It was said that the keel was winged. If so, it would be a radical departure from the traditional single-tab, shark-finned keel of other 12-Meters. Whether the rumour was true or not, two things were certain: Ben Lexcen, the design magician, was up to his old tricks, and the cunning Aussies were up to smoke-and-mirrors, sleight-of-hand intrigue.

But it was the very beginning of the campaign, and the boat had not yet been seen on the unyielding chop off Newport. This mysterious keel might be new; it might (God forbid!) even work. But four months of trial in battle lay ahead, dozens of races in all manner of sea and wind conditions, against yachts from France, England, Italy, Canada and two other challengers from Australia. One had to take into consideration, too, the fact that Lexcen had been experimenting with winged keels, dorsal fins and other fish-like appendages for years. Each experiment had ended in unmitigated failure. And there was Bob Bavier's statement about the unlikelihood of a breakthrough in the design of 12-Meters; that was pretty much the party line in the yachting world. Olin Stephens, the unchallenged king of 12-Meter design, had apparently perfected the art form. To deviate far from that was to invite disaster. Finally, there were one hundred and thirty-two years of history confronting the white boat from Down Under. There had to be more to her than a mysterious winged keel if she expected to pull off the upset of the century and beat the Americans.

But by mid-June, the mystery keel was no longer just a subject of curiosity and tolerant, good-natured speculation; *Australia II* found herself abruptly thrust onto the world stage. The America's Cup had become a global media event, and *Great White* from the land Down Under became front-page news. The boat rapidly found itself embroiled in controversy—thanks to the unseen and closely guarded keel. The sarong which covered it was a red flag waved in front of the international press corps and the New York Yacht Club, ever watchful for any threat to the America's Cup. To make matters more interesting (for the press) and more worrisome (for the New York Yacht Club), the Aussies, besides playing cloak-and-dagger with their keel, began to chock up race victories hand-over-fist. And they did not just win: They demolished their opponents, beating them by unheard of margins—hundreds of yards instead of five or six boat-lengths, minutes rather than seconds. It was, in the words of one headline, "The Summer Rampage of the *Great White.*" And the mighty New York Yacht Club was not amused.

Australia II's record in the first double round-robin series was eleven to one, a spectacular achievement. It scared the living daylights out of other challenge syndicates and the Americans, for the first time in the history of the America's Cup defense, were truly rattled. The myth of the superboat, of *Great White*, was born. Win or lose, she had already become the star of the twenty-fifth America's Cup challenge.

On Australia II sagging spirits and hope are revived . . . .

Red Dog and *Great White* are headed toward the buoy some three miles distant. They will soon round the marker and begin leg four, the second

Windshadow

weather leg. The unstable wind has shifted somewhat to the southeast, turning the third leg into more of a downwind run—the kind at which the Australian boat excels.

During this summer of inconstant and often feckless wind, a newspaper had run a tongue-in-cheek story about New England weather. Inspiration was drawn from Mark Twain: "There is a sumptuous variety about the New England weather, that compels admiration and regret. The weather is always doing something there; always attending strictly to business; always getting up new designs and trying them on the people to see how they will go . . . . I have counted one hundred and thirty-six different kinds of weather inside of four-and-twenty hours." Twain's laconic humor had caused many a Newport sailor to smile and nod his head in heartfelt agreement. But on board the 12-Meters, crew members are too absorbed in the search for elusive wings of wind to appreciate humor in weather conditions that are, by their very nature, capricious and cruel. And, in keeping with this nature, faithful, certain wind remains frustratingly out of reach.

Today, because of the umbrella phenomenon created by the spectator craft, what wind there is remains spoiled and patchy. The sea, too, is disturbed by the drifting wash of a thousand churning propellers. Pockets of warm air waft by, the rearguard of a summer in retreat, followed by a sudden chill heralding the advance of fall.

Finally, freshening breezes arrive but they avow no loyalty. For a moment, the wind is an ally of the red boat, then of the white. Here *Great White* gains twenty yards, there *Red Dog* hungrily snatches them back. For several minutes, this see-saw battle continues, the Americans hanging on to their hard-fought lead. But finally, as if tired of the game, the wind chooses the Australians. *Great White*'s green and gold spinnaker, which has been wobbling in the uncertain wind, hardens, and the boat settles resolutely in the water to begin shaving seconds off *Red Dog*'s lead.

Dennis Conner is gifted with a superb sense of time and distance. Computer-like, his mind rapidly processes relative boat speeds and distance to the buoy-marker. "They will cut our lead by half," he quietly announces to Tom Whidden, his tactician. At 3:10 p.m. *Red Dog* rounds the buoy, followed twenty-three seconds later by *Great White*. Conner's calculations have been dead on: Bertrand has sliced the American lead exactly in half.

2:45 pm

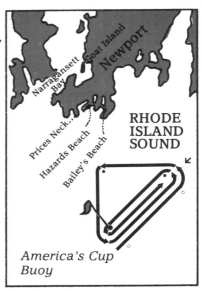

Narragansett Bay

Goat Island

Newport

Prices Neck

Hazards Beach

Bailey's Beach

RHODE ISLAND SOUND

America's Cup Buoy

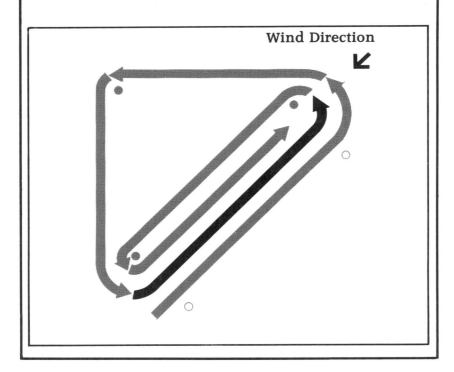

Wind Direction

The Fourth Leg

To keep heart when all have lost it; to go through intrigue
spotless . . . . who can say this is not greatness?

Thackeray

On Rhode Island Sound a sea mist has
begun to form. The boats are out of the chop
created by the spectator fleet, and although the
wind is truer it begins to soften. It drops in a
single minute from fifteen knots to a moderate
breeze of seven or eight. And there for several
moments it stays, not spoiling or shifting. For
once on this long afternoon, the wind is stable in
strength and direction.

John Bertrand calls for a sail change. The
genoa, the large headsail that overlaps the mainsail, is dropped. A light-wind genoa is hoisted in
its place. The change takes fifty seconds of
muscled clipping, hauling and hoisting. But it
suits *Great White*. She accelerates, inexorably
closing in on *Red Dog*. The next marker cannot be
seen in the mist, nor, suddenly, can land. In the
distance there is only a purple, shadowy horizon.

But *Red Dog* is dead ahead and *Great White* has a bead on her, a heat-seeking missile homing in on the hot exhaust of its unsuspecting target. Bertrand, in the midst of this critical moment of combat, is unaccountably suddenly conscious of the pleasant swish of water against hull, the sigh of wind in the rigging, the loud shudder of the great sails as they flex their muscles, golden in the light of a softly fading afternoon. The harmony of sound, light, color and water is a lyrical poem to his sailor's heart. Yet, he has no time for such thoughts. He is closing fast on *Red Dog*. The two hulls are separated by no more than a boat length. The predatory *Great White* dispassionately moves in for the kill. *Red Dog* is paralyzed.

In another hundred years or so, Rhode Island may be, perhaps, as pretty as the Isle of Wight.

Trollope (1862)

Newport has long been America's pre-eminent summer retreat for the unimaginably wealthy. Families such as the Vanderbilts and the Astors brought with them, when they came at the turn of the century, incomes that could be counted on to exceed expenditures by prodigiously large margins. Their New York mansions were palatial, as were their French *châteaux*; their yachts and their Newport summer cottages were the last word in luxury. Cottages? Yes, those magnificent dwellings (Rosecliffe, Marble House, The Breakers, The Elms) that front Bellevue Avenue were called cottages—although to the average American they would truly be mansions or palaces, such is their architectural inspiration and magnificence.

The contest to outspend income in those heady, Gilded Age days was a desperate one, a race that the very rich seemed destined to lose from the outset; investments were cresting to unheard-of levels of return, and the financial tide seemed always to be at the high-water mark.

At Newport, for the season of 1902, Grace and Cornelius Vanderbilt rented *Beaulieu*, the cottage of the William Waldorf Astors. There, Mrs. Vanderbilt staged a truly opulent—some would say decadent—*affaire de luxe*. "I have never even dreamt of such luxury," Grand Duke Boris, a visiting Russian nobleman and guest, incredulously told an American friend, Harry Lehr. "Is this really America, or have I landed on an enchanted island? Such an outpouring of riches! It is like walking on gold. We have nothing to equal it in Russia. Mr. Lehr, you will have to come over to Europe to show us how you conjure up all these visions of splendor." For her *fête*, Grace Vanderbilt transported from Broadway the entire cast and scenery of a popular musical comedy *The Wild Rose*. For five days before the extravagant affair, two carpentry crews and one shift of electricians worked day and night to construct a temporary theater on the grounds of *Beaulieu*. Inside the mansion, rooms and parlors were strewn with thousands of American Beauty roses. Their fragrance left a lasting impression: The party went down in Newport's already glittering social history as the *Fête des Roses*.

During an earlier Newport season, Alva Vanderbilt, wife of William Kissam Vanderbilt I (father of "Mike" Vanderbilt), had transformed the first floor of Marble House, with its soaring Corinthian columns the most striking of the Bellevue mansions, into a floral garden. A bronze fountain in the great entrance hall became the focal point of an African water *tableau*, and hyacinths mingled with lotus of the Nile around the splashing, sparkling water. A swarm of painted hummingbirds hovered amid real flowers and guests looked twice—not quite certain whether the birds might be alive. In an adjacent bower, pale hollyhocks rose high above the golden floor, surrounded by giant three-dimensional butterflies and bees that, despite their size, looked no less alive than did the hummingbirds. On the ocean side of the mansion (where in 1914 Alva, now remarried to O.H.P. Morgan, would construct an elaborate pagoda teahouse), thirty tables were artfully placed to catch the caress of summer breezes. The entire lawn—five acres—was transformed into a courtyard bounded by potted palms and tree ferns imported for the occasion.

It was not, however, a world in which all was peace and harmony. The sad but forthright sentiment of Alva's first husband, "Willie" Kissam Vanderbilt, was that money cannot buy happiness. Money only left this man "with nothing to hope for, with nothing definite to seek or strive for." "Inherited wealth," Vanderbilt said, "is a real handicap to happiness. It is as certain death to ambition as cocaine is to morality."

Newport and the America's Cup are inextricably linked; and while many of the ultra-wealthy summer residents are content to watch the races and host the parties, some become more involved in the competitive spirit. "Willie" Kissam Vanderbilt participated in the funding of various America's Cup syndicates during the early years of this century. And his son, Harold "Mike" Vanderbilt, escaped his father's monumental cynicism to attain lasting fame as a great yacht racer. The younger Vanderbilt—who also invented contract bridge—drafted the International Yacht Racing rules that today continue to govern nearly every sailing competition world-wide. He also donated Marble House to the Newport Preservation Society in 1963; it now contains an America's Cup Memorial Room bearing his name. The room is dominated by a portrait of "Mike" at the wheel of *Ranger* (1937), the last and swiftest of the huge J-class Cup racers.

During a Cup summer, every Newport socialite is in her element. It is a season of gala balls, *après*-midnight dinners, staggering fireworks displays, clambakes and dancing on dew-kissed lawns to the music of live orchestras. It is also a season of royalty. The summer of 1983 featured Prince Andrew (then one of the world's most eligible bachelors), Prince and Princess Michael of Kent, the Aga Khan with his wife, Salimah, and his half-sister, Princess Yasmin Aga Khan, daughter of American film actress Rita Hayworth and Prince Aly Khan.

In an America's Cup summer full of highlights, there is one social event that stands above the rest: the America's Cup Ball. It is held in The Breakers, Newport's grandest mansion, built for Cornelius Vanderbilt in 1895. The entrance to the buff Indiana limestone palace is through wrought iron gates that weigh seven tons and stretch thirty feet high at the center. Inside, the Great Hall rises over fifty feet to an upper floor loggia that offers a breathtaking view of ocean surf exploding against a rocky promontory.

On August 20th the *crème-de-la-crème* of Newport society, the New York Yacht Club and the competing 12-Meter syndicates, gathered at The Breakers. Among the guests were members of *Australia II*'s brain-trust—the Alan Bonds, the Warren Joneses and the Sir James Hardys. Conspicuous by their absence were John and Rasa Bertrand. The skipper from each 12-Meter yacht had been invited but tickets were strictly limited to six per syndicate. Sir James—John Bertrand's predecessor as helmsman of the Australian Cup challenger—had exercised the prerogative of his peerage and usurped the Bertrands' invitation.

Alan Bond's behavior on this most grand of

America's Cup social events was impeccable; he was the perfect gentleman. The fact did not go undetected by those who had been part of the Cup's social history for the last few decades. Bond's deportment redeemed him in the eyes of a Newport society that had looked askance at his brash entrance to their rarefied world in 1974. But although Bond was gracious beyond reproach, he was still viewed by Newport society with a curiously anxious eye. For not only was *Australia II* a threat on Rhode Island Sound, it posed a threat on land as well. If it were to defeat the American defender it would deprive Newport society of its triennial golden orgy: the America's Cup social season. And so, as the guests danced under the stars to the music of the Roland Haas Orchestra, there were guarded premonitions that they were witness to the end of an era.

Double, double toil and trouble.   *Shakespeare*

The New York Yacht Club had done everything possible to stop *Great White*—everything short of sabotage, or so the common Newport watering-hole wisecrack went. They had questioned her paternity, suggesting that Ben Lexcen had not designed *Australia II* alone, that the Netherlands Aerospace Laboratory and Netherlands Ship Model Basin (where Lexcen had worked for four months), had taken a hand in the mysterious keel design. If the charge were true, the Australians would be in direct violation of the race's constitution. The Deed of Gift stipulates that the design of all 12-Meters competing in the America's Cup must be the creation solely of the challenging country.

In the paranoia of the summer—a paranoia that

leapfrogged ahead every time *Great White* won a race—the Dutch and Lexcen were seen as co-conspirators in a diabolical plot, the sole intent of which was to deprive the New York Yacht Club of the America's Cup.

Just as the keels of the competing boats sliced through the sea, so this American paranoia sliced through reason, discretion and prudence. It would ravage the image of the New York Yacht Club and tear to shreds the credibility of the club's America's Cup committee. The committee dispatched a telex to the Netherlands that read, in part: "I understand you and your team are responsible for development and design of the special keel for *Australia II*. We are finally convinced of her potential and would therefore like to build same design under one of our boats." The telex was authored by Ed du Moulin, head of *Liberty*'s syndicate.

Ostensibly its purpose was to elicit some technical knowledge about the keel. That alone was sufficient reason for the Australians to cry foul, but the first sentence was tantamount to a declaration of war. It suggested as a *fait accompli* Dutch complicity in the design of the keel.

The Dutch did not rise to the bait. They replied: "We have received your telex . . . and would ask you to note firstly that we were associated with the *Australia II* campaign by way of a tank-testing contract. Their designer, Mr. Ben Lexcen, resided at Wageningen for four months whilst he completed the design for both *Australia II* and *Challenge 12*.

"As we are contracted to them not to test 12-Meter models for any other 12-Meter syndicate until the completion of the 1983 campaign, we have today advised them of your query and requested their permission to undertake work for you. But unfortunately they have advised us that they are not prepared to allow such dispensation. We thank you for your enquiry and would be only too delighted to discuss work for you related to any campaign in 1986."

The Australians, particularly Ben Lexcen, were incensed. Lexcen interpreted the American telex as a direct assault on his reputation as a yacht designer. He is a man of genial disposition, more given to good-natured repartee than to verbal fisticuffs. It was he who had set Newport laughing with the irreverent comment that if the Australians won the Cup they would steamroller it and call it the America's Plate. But the controversy about whether he was indeed the sole father of the white boat's design momentarily effaced his even temper and good humor. The American telex made him long instead to steamroller the America's Cup committee.

The Australian syndicate made the damaging (and potentially defamatory) American telex and the Dutch response available to the press—and the press had a field day. "Keelgate," trumpeted newspaper headlines in New York, London, Amsterdam (the Dutch having suddenly found themselves embroiled in America's Cup controversy), Paris, Rome—and in the land Down Under. Australia's dailies ran riot with the story.

The Americans pleaded (or feigned) innocence; the Australians charged mendacious and unsportsmanlike subterfuge. The jury, the world press, convicted the Americans. Yet before the long summer was over, the New York Yacht Club would be embarrassed by still more controversy, for what had developed into a public relations nightmare was far from over; it rapidly became a farce worthy of Molière.

Since the Dutch would not play ball, other steps would be taken to obtain information about the keel. But how to manage that? It was a nettlesome problem. Consideration was given to photographing *Great White* from the air when she was heeling over, thus revealing

Winged Keel

the keel just beneath the water's surface. It seemed feasible, and arrangements for chartering a plane were made. But fate intervened. On the appointed day the wind would not co-operate, and the white boat could not heel over. The *Liberty* syndicate's strategem died with that day's wind.

The Australians themselves were subject to the general paranoia although perhaps with more justification. To be safe they had painted a false keel on the winged keel to foil the efforts of airborne Peeping Toms. In order to thwart more sophisticated means of espionage they also circulated the rumor that the hull and keel of their boat were equipped with electronic sensors and spoilers. In fact, the sensors and spoilers did not exist.

Members of the *Liberty* syndicate were nothing if not inventive. They reasoned that if espionage by air would not work, an amphibious approach might. They decided on a frogman. The scenario was simple enough: The diver would be positioned at one of the marks where the white boat would be doing a hundred-and-eighty degree turn and thus be at her slowest—in fact virtually stationary for a brief instant. As she slowed, the diver would snap pictures from an underwater camera. It seemed like an entirely plausible solution to the tormenting dilemma of how to crack the super-keel mystery. But a snag immediately developed: No professional diver would undertake the assignment. It was considered too risky a proposition. Where was James Bond when you needed him? was the unspoken lament.

At this point, the *Red Dog* syndicate almost conceded defeat. Brief consideration was given to having a scuba diver swim into *Great White's* berth at Newport Offshore and, as the boat was being raised, pop up out of the water like a jack-in-the-box, take a few hasty snaps and duck back down into the safety of the murky harbor. But ethical qualms (which for some reason had not entered into earlier scheming) cancelled the plot.

Such considerations of conscience did not deter two Canadian divers—Frogman I and Frogman II. The first diver, identified as a boat driver for *Canada I*, was caught in the half-light of dawn in *Great White*'s berth at Newport Offshore. In his hand was an underwater camera. Unfortunately for the intruder, security guards had observed suspicious bubbles in the water beside the Australian boat. Mindful that Newport was now a war zone, the guards leaped into the oily harbor fully clothed. (It is amusing to note that these guards were Americans, not Australians. It is also a curious case of history repeating itself. These unsung heroes aided and abetted the Aussie enemy just as the English pilot aboard *America* helped defeat his own countrymen in 1851, when the Cup was first brought to America.) The Australians, somewhat unnerved by the episode, tightened security, enclosing their berth with a twelve-volt underwater electrical screen. Although the collared scuba diver was a Canadian, it was assumed that he was operating in league with covert American interests.

The second diver was never captured. It appeared he was a mercenary, armed not only with a camera but with a strong sense of business acumen. He first sold pen-and-ink representations of the keel, revealing himself as a showman by autographing the drawings simply as Frogman II. Later he apparently sold his negatives to the Toronto *Globe and Mail*. That newspaper first published pictures of the keel on the morning of September 26, 1983, the day of the final race.

After the two Canadian divers left the stage, the New York Yacht Club decided it would once and for all neutralize *Australia II*'s threat to the America's Cup. The club declared all-out war, mobilizing forces on several fronts. A counter-insurgency unit was recruited. It was called the Dutch Connection because the players were related to Johan Valentijn, *Liberty*'s designer, in one way or another: Wil Valentijn was an uncle and Antoon (Tony) J. van Rijn was a family friend residing in North Carolina. Van Rijn was in the fiberglass manufacturing business but was also quite knowledgeable about yacht design. He and Johan Valentijn had grown up together in the same village. Both had emigrated to America as adults. Wil Valentijn, like his nephew, possessed a more than passing knowledge of yacht design; he was a ship-wright.

Knowledge of yacht design was an essential prere-quisite for their mission: infiltration of the Dutch research facilities used by Ben Lexcen. The objective of this clandestine activity was to secure admissions from the Dutch who had worked with Lexcen that they, not he, had designed the radical keel. Failing this, they were at least to elicit some acknowledgement that the Dutch had had a meaningful part in the design.

These brave lads were to do their work cloaked in secrecy, but it was to be a secret ineptly kept.

Meanwhile the New York Yacht Club moved its heavy artillery to the public front, where it was already being mauled by an increasingly hostile press. The club fired a tactical weapon, a thirty-four-page missive, at the Australians. It contained the accusation that their boat was a 12.45-Meter, an illegal mutant, and must therefore be declared ineligible and shipped back to Australia.

Included in the missive was the following statement: "If the closely guarded peculiar keel design of *Australia II* is allowed to remain in competition, or is allowed to continue to be rated without penalty, the yacht will likely win the foreign trials and will likely win the America's Cup in September." This statement belonged to Halsey Herreshoff. Though a naval architect like his grandfather before him, the legendary Herreshoff blood was not Halsey's only connection to the America's Cup; he was the navigator for *Liberty*. He summed up the situation regarding the Australian keel in terms a hitherto untutored but now very interested public could understand: "What we have here is a bunch of apples and one orange."

It was this statement, more than any other in the lengthy document, that was red-flagged by the America's Cup world. This statement dared give voice to the unthinkable: that the America's Cup would leave the New York Yacht Club, and the United States, after a hundred and thirty-two years. There had, of course, been such talk all summer long. *Great White* had been destroying its opposition until nothing stood between it and the Cup—except *Red Dog*. But here, in public, a member of the New York Yacht Club syndicate, the last line of defense, was already anticipating defeat. The Australians were astounded at this revelation. My God! They had been daring themselves to think the unthinkable for many months, ever since *Freedom's* smashing of *Australia* three years before. Every day there was a litany to be repeated: *Believe the Cup can be ours. We can win. We can win. We can win . . . .* Like a monastic chant it had penetrated the subconscious of every member of John Bertrand's crew. Herreshoff's disclosure confirmed the Australian mindset: They *could* win the Cup. At the same time it unnerved Dennis Conner's crew considerably. All of a sudden the dread realization penetrated: We could *lose* the Cup.

The committee's "legal" weapon proved to be a dud—or, perhaps more appropriately, a boomerang. It turned course, came right back at the New York Yacht Club and detonated in the committee's face.

Every boat is measured prior to the Cup competition to ensure conformity with the 12-Meter rule. Every other syndicate may have a representative present at a competitor's measuring. The measurement of *Australia II* was carried out on June 16th (two days before competition began) at Cove Haven Marina, not far from Newport. The New York Yacht Club knew of the place and time but, somehow, in an incredible slip-up, no one from the club was present at the measurement. And the three-man international committee (John Savage, an Australian, Tony Watts, an Englishman, and Mark Vinbury, an American) responsible for supervising compliance with the 12-Meter rule unanimously certified the white boat as being a legal 12-Meter.

Vinbury (a member of the New York Yacht Club) was later vilified in some quarters as being unpatriotic. Should he not have discarded his oath of confidentiality and at least tipped off the U.S. America's Cup syndicates as to the unique design feature of the Australian boat's keel? Or even taken a further step and declared the keel illegal? But Vinbury did not bend in the face of such intimidation. Rulings by the measurement committee are deemed final and binding within the yacht-racing establishment. The ruling that *Australia II* was a legal challenger remained unanimous.

The Dutch connection also came up empty-handed. They had attempted to have the Amsterdam test tank experts sign affidavits stating that Lexcen had not been the sole impetus behind the design of the winged keel. This skullduggery backfired. The angry Dutch chief of research sent a telex confirming that he and his facilities had "acted solely pursuant to Mr. Lexcen's directions at all times." He further advised that the support his team had provided was "similar to the computer support work and tank testing provided by the Delft University of Technology here to the designer of *Magic* and *Liberty*—Johan Valentijn." It was a perfect case of point/counterpoint.

At this juncture the prudent approach for the New York Yacht Club would have been to make a low-profile exit, however ignominious. The Cup committee had been, in the words of more than one journalist present in Newport, a tempest full of sound and fury—and not much more. Instead, behind a demeanor composed of one part indignation and one part self-righteousness, the committee continued with a cause already lost. Committee members were convinced they were guardians charged with ensuring the sanctity of the Deed of Gift. It was their solemn duty, they maintained, to ensure fair play—not just for the Americans but for the other competitors as well. The New York Yacht Club's Commodore Stone stated the situation thus: "I think you should realize that this Cup comes under a Deed of Gift. There are conditions for the Cup races that you know. And we feel an obligation—not only to our own defending syndicates but to other challenging syndicates—when there are some reports that possibly contravene the Deed of Gift, we feel an obligation to check into it." The committee asked members of the Australian syndicate—on the eve of the match of the century—to sign papers to the effect that they had indeed complied with the 12-Meter rule, and that their boat conformed to the terms of the Deed of Gift. The Australians, not surprisingly, refused to sign such a statement, being under no legal compulsion to do so.

The night before the *Australia II—Liberty* match the America's Cup committee convened on board Bus Mosbacher's luxury yacht, generals on the eve of battle, and despite their steadfast conviction that *Australia II* was illegal, despite unwavering indignation and self-righteousness, there was a pervasive sense that they had already lost a battle and would soon be losing the war as well. They had, of course, a last minute draconian option—declare *Australia II* illegal and damn the consequences. But the anticipated world-wide repercussions of such a decision were too horrific to contemplate. No. They were trapped in a conundrum of their own making. And the truth was simple in its finality: No retreat availed itself.

Great White dispassionately moves in for the kill . . .

On board *Red Dog,* Dennis Conner and his crew can actually hear the approach of *Great White* as it glides through the water, as purposefully as a shark led by the bloody spoor of a disabled prey. Yet the slap of waves against hull possesses a strangely rhythmic cadence, like the oar stroke of an ancient galley. The sound is hypnotic, almost immobilizing.

Conner is momentarily transfixed. He steels himself for the final attack. If he and *Red Dog* are overtaken, all is lost. For the next leg is the downwind run—the run on which *Great White* has consistently shown an excellence that Conner knows with chilling certainty *Red Dog* cannot match. But in this moment of despair, this moment when defeat is at hand . . . unbelievably, an angel of mercy descends from the heavens. The angel is a sailor's dream, a header—a powerful sustaining wind that feeds directly into the sails.

John Bertrand, on board *Australia II,* is aghast. He is speechless. He was about to deliver a blow from which he knew the Americans could not possibly recover and suddenly, out of the still air, as if Dennis Conner had dialed it up, comes this fresh, powerful blast of wind. He can hear his

Sail Change

tactician, Hughey Treharne, repeating over and over again: *I just cannot believe this . . . . I just cannot believe this . . . .*

Conner cannot believe it either. He had felt the cold breath of death on his cheek, only to be handed another life—all within a single, crucial second. And this wind appears to be no transient savior. It has taken *Red Dog* on its powerful shoulders and with enormous strength carried it forward. Conner's amazement is matched only by his boundless and fervent prayers of gratitude. God is an American! He has proved Himself to be a vacillating, pitiless God, for He has tortured *Red Dog* as He is now torturing *Great White*. But all that matters now is that this life-saving wind has filled the American sails.

Dennis Conner is not unmindful of the criticism directed his way by those who do not subscribe to his do-or-die approach to the Cup. But victory on this day will silence every critic. For it is accepted wisdom in Newport that *Australia II* is the faster craft. Only two men in Cup history, Mike Vanderbilt (*Rainbow*, 1934) and Bus Mosbacher (*Weatherly*, 1962) have defeated challengers generally acknowledged to be swifter than the American defender. Now such a triumph lies within his grasp.

The marker denoting the end of the fourth leg suddenly looms out of the mist, a beacon of burning orange. *Red Dog* is loping along like an ocean greyhound. Every hundred yards it seems to gain half a boat length. For several minutes, hundred-yard dash follows hundred-yard dash, each won by the American 12-Meter. It is Bertrand's turn to be immobilized, helpless in the face of this unspeakable fate. The Cup, which it seemed moments before he could reach out and touch, is receding into the distance, held tantalizingly aloft by *Red Dog*. He watches as the Americans whip around the marker and smartly run up their giant parachute spinnaker. It immediately inflates with wind and *Liberty* is off.

Bertrand steals a glance at Conner. The boats, heading in opposite directions, are separated by no more than thirty yards. Conner does not return Bertrand's look—if he has noticed it at all. His lips, smeared with white zinc sunscreen ointment, are set in a thin line; the grim set of his opponent's face raises Bertrand's spirits. There is no curve of triumph on those lips. Conner is obviously concerned, despite his huge lead.

And then, in the blink of an eye, *Great White* is at the marker and Bertrand must turn his attention to matters at hand. He swings the wheel around hard. The Australian boat responds instantly, careening around the marker in a fluid, sideswiping motion. With practised skill the crew runs up a mammoth spinnaker of pure white. The sail blossoms and then, balloon-like, lifts *Great White* over every resistant ocean swell.

Bertrand's navigator, Grant Simmer, delivers the news the Australian helmsman dreads but must hear: The Americans have a fifty-seven second lead. Only once before has *Red Dog* been so far in front of *Great White*.

3:33 pm

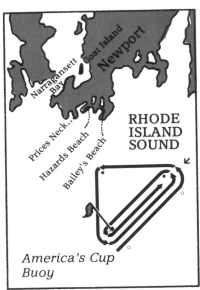

Narragansett Bay

Goat Island

Newport

Prices Neck

Hazards Beach

Bailey's Beach

RHODE ISLAND SOUND

America's Cup Buoy

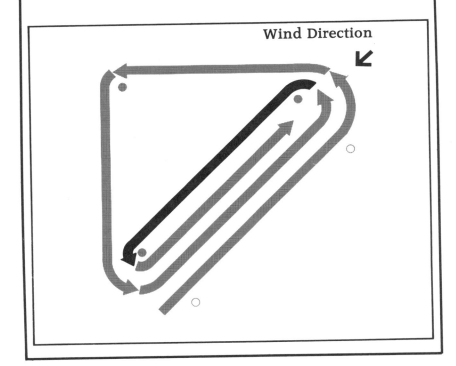

Wind Direction

The Fifth Leg

If you want to know what it is to feel the "correct" social world fizzle to nothing, you should come to Australia. It is a weird place. In the **established** *sense it is socially nil. Happy-go-lucky, don't-you-bother, we're-in-Australia. But also there seems to be no inside life of any sort: just a long lapse and drift. A rather fascinating indifference . . . . the spell of indifference gets to me.*

D.H. Lawrence

As he rounds the mark for the downwind leg, John Bertrand's mind is a kaleidoscope of images and emotions. It seems he is reliving his life as does a drowning man. His mind is a slide projector gone berserk, flashing back to . . . click! Twenty-two Bristol Avenue, the little red-shingled house on Port Phillip Bay where he had grown up . . . click! His first summer at Newport, 1970, and the Aussies' losing boat, *Gretel II* . . . .

But the images stop at a single frame, featuring a pale blond blue-eyed East German, Jochen Schumann. Schumann's cold, appraising eyes are flickering on and off Bertrand. The East German is perhaps a dozen feet behind the Australian as both men plane at high speed over the green waters of Lake Ontario in single-man Finn-class sailboats, in the sixth race of the 1976 Olympic regatta. Schumann is first in the standings, Bertrand second. For both men the gold medal is a single victory away.

Schumann's eyes are those of a professional, a man who has been through the drill before and is possessed of total self-control. Those cold, unblinking eyes unnerve Bertrand. Can I escape him? Outrun him? But Bertrand cannot seem to shake the East German's eyes and—as if by telepathy—their passionless, cold-blooded stare capsizes his boat.

Actually, Bertrand—rattled—had made a rash move to reposition his mainsheet; the sail had slipped from his hands, tossing the boat over and throwing Bertrand into the drink. And the remarkable thing was that those eyes had not been on Bertrand for longer than an instant. They had been on the water and the wind, concentrating on winning. Jochen Schumann captured the gold medal while John Bertrand had to settle for the bronze. It was a lesson Bertrand would never forget. For one brief second the East German had caused him, poised as he was for victory, to question whether he was good enough. He had paid a high price for that doubt. But in return, Bertrand had learned a cardinal rule of competition: Never panic. Do nothing on impulse. Be calm, be cool, be rational. Be Jochen Schumann's eyes: cold-blooded and efficient.

Red Dog has a fifty-seven second lead . . . .

Bertrand's eyes dispassionately appraise the hated *Red Dog* sixty to seventy yards off the bow of *Great White*. The American boat is bowling over the ocean, propelled by the same header that carried it beyond the grasp of the Australian boat at the end of the fourth leg. But Bertrand has recovered from the initial shock of seeing the American boat snatched from his grasp by the invisible hand of the wind. His mood now is not one of self-doubt. There are two legs to run—more than eight miles—at least another hour of racing. The America's Cup is still there for the taking.

On board *Black Swan*, the white boat's tender, the mood is far from cautious optimism. Ben Lexcen cannot endure the agony of seeing his latest progeny follow in the path of defeated *Southern Cross* and *Australia*. He disappears below deck with sailmaker Tom Schnackenberg, who is himself shaken. For Lexcen the sluice gate of repressed memories opens, and in flood a hundred images of past defeats at the hands of American 12-Meters. In his mind a roll call sounds: *Gretel*, 1962; *Dame Pattie*, 1967; *Gretel II*, 1970; *Southern Cross*, 1974; *Australia*, 1977; *Australia* again, 1980. Many of these defeats were massacres. The Americans won seventeen of twenty races, and in the 1977 contest, not only did they win four to nil but their boat *Courageous*, captained by Ted Turner, beat *Australia* on every leg. Twenty-four legs, twenty-four American victories. And now it appears that, despite heroic Australian efforts, there will be a new addition to the roll call of defeated America's Cup challengers: *Australia II*, 1983.

On board *Fox Hunter II* the mood is distinctly more upbeat. As *Red Dog* rounded the marker with her commanding lead, fists were raised in unrestrained glee. The Cup is safe! It has been, as Wellington said at

Waterloo, "a close-run thing." Those crafty, pugnacious, persevering Australians have given the New York Yacht Club a testing run for their money. Every member of the America's Cup committee has been severely jolted by the boat from the land Down Under. But justice does exist on the race course, and today justice has prevailed. *Great White*, with her super-keel, her illicit mutation, has been struck down by their champion, Dennis Conner. Let the acrimony of the summer of 1983 be put behind them.

Inevitably, there would be post-mortem repercussions, despite *Red Dog*'s last-minute victory. But the Cup committee members are realists: In the final analysis, winning is the name of the game. It has been a snakes-and-ladders summer, but in the end they have won. And as victors they can deflect any criticism of their behavior and conduct. Perhaps they have been a trifle heavy-handed. But what the press and the rest of the world have forgotten, as they eagerly lap up the accusations and counter-charges surrounding the New York Yacht Club, is the sacred trust placed in the committee's hands, the Deed of Gift that commands strict fair play. What the committee knows and everyone else either cannot or will not see is that the Aussies, with their winged keel, have—here the committee must choose their words with care—*possibly* bent the rules. It is the cunning Aussies who are to blame for the scandal-plagued summer. The Australians are, in short, a clan of troublemakers.

Already the committee's collective mind is focused not only on savoring victory an hour hence but on the 1987 defense. The mistakes of 1983 will not be repeated. The challengers, especially the Australians, will never again be permitted to get so close to their lady, the beloved Cup. She belongs to the New York Yacht Club; she belongs in her temple on West 44th Street.

This sense of miraculously staved-off defeat is not shared by the men on *Liberty*. In spite of their boat's lead of almost a minute, there is a definite air of foreboding. Each man in the afterguard—Dennis Conner, tactician Tom Whidden and navigator Halsey Herreshoff—had, before leaving the dockside that morning, arrived at the theoretical lead that would be necessary to fight off *Great White*'s final charge, the all-out assault that they knew *Red Dog* would have to withstand. Each man had deduced a different figure, but among them the smallest predetermined lead time deemed necessary for victory was seventy-five seconds. *Great White* is now within fifty-seven seconds of *Red Dog*.

Lowliness is young ambition's ladder.   *Shakespeare*

In 1974, the America's Cup cast of characters—already quite extraordinary by any standard—was augmented by yet another colorful player: Alan Bond.

Bond had come to Australia from London after World War II, when the empty island continent had opened her doors to all who could afford the twenty-pound cost of a sea ticket from the U.K. The Second World War had brought home to Australia how truly isolated and defenseless she was, and so her government had instituted the "twenty-pound" program as a way of adding to her population.

Australians call newcomers to their country "migrants," and the word has unmistakably pejorative overtones. It calls to the Aussie mind a semiliterate, unskilled laborer, equipped to face the new world with only callus-hardened hands and gritty determination.

Most migrants make it to the middle class, but very few go beyond. The dynamics of Australian society are such that the migrant trying to achieve and prosper is faced with a strange paradox. It is possible, if a person is possessed of sufficient ambition, drive and talent, to climb to the very top. But the social climber will have to overcome a uniquely Australian obstacle—the middle-class affinity for averageness. The Australian middle class will be tugging at the migrant's shirtsleeves. The message is: Don't strive for the top; be satisfied with the *status quo*. While the United States worships ambition and craves success, Australia debunks both. The achievements of Alan Bond, a true Australian migrant, are therefore all the more remarkable.

An adolescent Bond, with his family, left a lower-class east-end London suburb for Australia, arriving in Fremantle, south of Perth. In many ways Fremantle, Western Australia's major harbor, is the Aussies' Ellis Island. In the 1950s, immigrants flooded in as half a century before they had streamed into America in the shadow of the Statue of Liberty.

Eventually, Bond became a millionaire land developer and yacht racer—but wealth and power did not come easily. Like many of his contemporaries in the world of America's Cup challengers, Bond started his working life humbly. In the tradition of Baron Marcel Bich—the French pen magnate who challenged for the Cup from 1970 to 1980 and who had once sold lamps door to door—and of Peter de Savary—the British multimillionaire who brought the *Victory '83* team to Newport in 1983 and who was once an itinerant encyclopedia salesman—Bond painted signs for a living before his fortunes changed. An example of his handiwork can still be seen in Fremantle. It is advertisement for the Great Southern Roller Flour Mills, an illustration of a large red dog on a white background.

Bond's first challenge for the America's Cup was in 1974. The challenge was announced through the Royal Perth Yacht Club amid a fanfare of promotion for Bond's latest land development, Sun City at Yanchep, on the Indian Ocean north of Perth.

Sun City nicely illustrates Alan Bond's drive and his ability to see potential in the most unlikely places. Prior to development as a resort community, it was an inhospitable area, the terrain pockmarked with sandhills, the only vegetation arthritic, low-lying scrub brush, spinifex grass and desiccated acacia trees. But the uninviting landscape, the unbearable heat and flies the size of wasps did not detract from Bond's determination. He bought the land for a song and proceeded to sell his vision to investors. He even had some of the sandhills painted green to counteract the area's total lack of aesthetic appeal. The chicanery worked. He was able to sell this arid piece of land to foreign interests.

Bond's 1974 America's Cup challenger, *Southern Cross,* was a forerunner of *Australia II* in two ways. Not only was she designed by the innovative Ben Lexcen, but she was built in great secrecy in a bushland factory near Sydney and transported across the continent to Fremantle covered with a tinfoil and tarpaulin shroud—the tinfoil to stop infra-red film being used by "American spies" to photograph her hull.

When at last the hull was unveiled, it became obvious that Lexcen had expanded on the hydrodynamic hull shapes used successfully with his ocean racers *Gingko* and *Apollo III.* A big-bodied boat with a smallish rig, *Southern Cross* was designed to be at her fastest in moderate to fresh winds, the winds that prevail on Rhode Island Sound.

Bond entered the America's Cup world—and Newport society—like a junkyard dog picking a fight with a feisty pedigreed terrier. The result was bared

teeth and an inordinate amount of snarling and bark-
ing. To some Newport observers, it seemed the
Australian went out of his way to antagonize the New
York Yacht Club and American yachtsmen everywhere.

In some ways Bond was following in the footsteps of
his predecessor, the volatile Sir Frank Packer, a man
who held no affection for the New York Yacht Club. During the 1970 *Gretel II—Intrepid* Cup match, Packer's
12-Meter defeated the American yacht in race two. But
after the race *Gretel II* was disqualified by the Club's
race committee for fouling *Intrepid* at the start-line, and
the American boat was declared the winner. Packer was
incensed at the decision, despite a consensus among
knowledgable yachtsmen that the verdict was the correct one. Packer raged that complaining to the New York
Yacht Club was like a husband complaining about his
wife to his mother-in-law.

The 1974 Cup campaign was a fiasco for Bond;
Southern Cross lost four to nil to America's *Courageous*.
It was not on Rhode Island Sound, however, that Bond
made his name in Newport during that first summer in
America, it was in the protest room that this combative
Australian displayed his disputatious nature. He had
brought with him an attorney who spent weeks boning
up on the Deed of Gift and the rules pertaining to the
Cup. Bond lost his protests but earned his reputation as
a force to be reckoned with.

Three years later, he returned with *Australia*, a boat
that was the result of a collaboration between Lexcen
and Johan Valentijn. But this time Bond's behavior was
exemplary. When asked why he kept returning to
Newport, he came up with a surprisingly statesmanlike
answer. "You get out there," he said, "and you're as
good as the next guy, who might be a Vanderbilt. You
get out there and all you've got is a common
element—the wind and the sea—and everybody's

equal." There were no more screams about the New York Yacht Club's defender enjoying privileged status over the challenger.

Unfortunately for Bond, this diplomatic behavior did not help on the water. *Australia* was destroyed by *Courageous*, skippered by Ted Turner. Bond's record was now zero to eight against the Americans.

The Australian millionaire and an extensively revamped *Australia* returned to challenge again in 1980, and again the Americans defended successfully, this time with Dennis Conner at the helm of *Freedom*. But somehow the challenge was different that summer, and for just a moment before the races were done the prescient could almost hear the Cup begin to rattle the bolt securing it to its plinth in the West 44th Street home of the New York Yacht Club.

The first shock came as *Freedom* was leading in the second race, only to have *Australia* overtake her by several hundred yards when the wind died. The Americans were saved at the last minute, however; the race was called because of the expiration of the five-hour-and-fifteen-minute time limit.

But for the Americans the worst was yet to come. The resailing of that second race proved to be one of the most exciting contests in the history of the America's Cup. On the first weather leg, *Australia* outpointed and outfooted *Freedom* and won by almost half a minute. On the first power reach, *Freedom* regained the lead when the Australians selected the wrong spinnaker. But the Australians quickly changed sails and passed *Freedom* to lead by a boat length at the mark, adding a further thirty seconds on the second weather leg. The downwind leg gave Conner his chance, as *Australia* sailed too far to the right. At the end of the downwind run, the Americans were two boat lengths ahead, with one leg to sail. In an intense tactical duel, *Australia* broke away from Conner's close cover halfway up that final leg, and in the approaching gloom of nightfall an Australian challenger won an America's Cup race for the first time in ten years.

But Dennis Conner threatened to drag the Americans into disgrace. Although he had been cleanly beaten, he lodged a protest grieving the absence of navigation lights on *Australia* during the post-sunset finish of the race. The protest smelled of sour grapes and pettiness. It was later withdrawn.

At the end of the summer of 1980, Bond's record was one and twelve. But he had learned a valuable lesson on this third Cup campaign, a lesson that would stand him in good stead on his fourth attempt, in 1983, to take the Cup Down Under. He now knew that the Americans were vulnerable, and he had seen Dennis Conner's reaction under the pressure of intense competition. The Australians left Newport in 1980 in a mood of quiet optimism, despite having won but a single race. Ben Lexcen was closing the gap between American and Australian design technology, and soon Tom Schnackenberg's sail-making expertise would effectively neutralize U.S. superiority in this vital area. Already a 1983 plan of attack was taking shape, based in part on doing psychological battle with Dennis Conner.

If a thing is humanly possible, consider it to be within your reach.   *Marcus Aurelius*

John Bertrand set out to win the America's Cup three years before the 1983 challenge. In fact, he could pinpoint the date—September 25th, 1980—and the moment—exactly 3:38 p.m.—when he knew he would challenge in 1983. It was the moment Dennis Conner and *Freedom* crossed the finish line to defeat *Australia* in the fifth and final race of 1980. The Australian boat, with Bertrand on board as a sail trimmer, followed three minutes, thirty-eight seconds later.

Unbeknown to Bertrand, Alan Bond had already committed himself to the 1983 challenge. Bertrand would also learn later that Bond had never held high hopes for the 1980 Australian challenge—that he viewed it more or less as a tune-up for the all-out assault to be mounted in 1983. Bond had not formulated future strategy, but he had chosen his key players: Ben Lexcen would again design the challenger and Warren Jones would again be syndicate manager. But Sir James Hardy, *Australia*'s helmsman, would be replaced by John Bertrand. This decision was made public by Bond—who had not bothered to consult Bertrand—on the afternoon of *Australia*'s defeat at the hands of *Freedom*. The news was relayed to Bertrand, still on board the losing Australian boat during its tow-back from the race course. At dockside in Newport, Bertrand formally accepted the promotion without a moment's hesitation. He had intuitively known that one day he would lead his countrymen in their bid to win the America's Cup.

Having dispensed with the formalities, Bertrand began—that very afternoon—plotting strategy for a campaign three years distant. If this seemed inconsistent with the situation at hand—the *Freedom* victory party was going strong all around the defeated Australians—it did not bother Bertrand. In fact, the boisterous celebration of *Freedom* and her supporters helped harden his resolve: Next time around it would be the joyous whooping of Australian voices washing over the somber, shell-shocked faces of the Americans.

But a battle plan does not emerge simply because the general has a strong resolve to win. The determination to defeat the Americans was easy enough to come by; but how to formulate an effective mode of attack?

Bertrand's mind is orderly, methodical and deductive, the analytical mind of an engineer. His approach to the 1983 Cup campaign evolved from this analytical way of thinking. Where were the Americans vulnerable? What were their weaknesses? How could those weaknesses be exploited? He examined the American sail program: their boat design, crew training, crew selection, morale, tactics (on and off the race course) and leadership—as well as the anticipated harassment tactics of the New York Yacht Club. At the same time, Bertrand assessed the weaknesses and strengths of the Australian camp. He fed all of these variables, some more tangible than others, into his own mental computer and out came the framework of a battle plan. Bertrand then set about adding substance to that frame.

The Australian plan of attack was multifaceted. The first part was predictable: development of the programs of physical and technical training necessary to whip the Australian crew and their boat into winning shape. Hours upon endless hours of practise sailing on the Indian and Pacific Oceans would result in attainment of the degree of stamina—and standard of competence—required to better the Americans.

The second and third prongs of the attack had next to nothing to do with sailing or yacht racing; they belonged to the realm of psychological warfare. Bertrand believed that to beat the Americans on Rhode Island Sound he had first to beat them in his mind, to believe utterly that he and his Australian crew could-destroy the Yanks.

The aura of America's power ranged far and wide—certainly to Australia, with its almost insignificant population of fifteen million. There was the aura, too, of history and tradition: The America's Cup had first been won when Australia had a population of less than a million, when convict labor was still being transported Down Under, courtesy of Her Majesty's penal system. In 1851, the year the Cup came to New York, Australia had not yet been crossed from south to north, or from east to west. It was like Mars: a red earth too hostile for exploring and certainly not a place for settling—save for social pariahs, ruffians, convicts, the discarded and disavowed of family and society—in general, the flotsam and jetsam of Victorian England. In 1851, Australia had a great deal of catching up to do before she could consider herself an equal of America, and in the minds of many Australians that was still the case in 1983.

Thus the work Bertrand had to do on the collective psyche of his men consisted of two elements: overcoming a hundred and thirty-two years of history and, more critically, overcoming the deeply ingrained Aussie inferiority complex.

Bertrand decided that this challenge, the twenty-fifth in America's Cup history, had to be treated in isolation from every other challenge. This was to be the foundation of the training of *Great White*'s crew. No crew member would be permitted to glance back over his shoulder at the America's Cup challenge record of twenty-four attempts and twenty-four dismal failures. In particular, no reference was to be made to the fact that of those twenty-four failures, six had been suffered by Australian yachtsmen, and that those six resounding defeats had occurred in the last twenty years of Cup competition. In Bertrand's mind, the reason the Cup had stayed in the New York Yacht Club was clear: The Americans had been better prepared every time, in yacht and sail design and in crew training. There was no magic formula to their success; they had simply put good men in good boats and gone out and beaten the best the world could muster in challenge.

Bertrand's second hurdle was uniquely Australian;

it had to do with his homeland's self-image. For much of the country's short history, Australians have thought of themselves as terrestrial Martians (or, in the vernacular of Australia, "Ockers") because of their separation from the mainstream of civilization by vast ocean reaches, reaches that, until the advent of the jet plane, were almost as distant as the light-years of space.

Ocker (there is no certain derivation of the word) is the equivalent of the Canadian Canuck, the British Tommy, the American Yankee. And Ocker, like Yank, has come to be a friendly, slap-on-the-back sort of sobriquet, certainly no longer a derisive label suggesting that Aussies are ill-bred and uncultured. But there still exists in the Australian character an Ocker-knocker tendency.

In the words of one Aussie-observer, the perfectly balanced Australian is one with two chips on his shoulder: his own inferiority complex and the observer's assumed condescension towards all things Australian. Aussie-to-Aussie each might be an Ocker; but Aussie-to-Yank is a different matter. John Bertrand and others have called it the "tall poppy syndrome," the Aussie habit of cutting down to size any countryman who out-achieves his neighbors.

And there was another danger—that a crew member, during an involuntary crisis of self-doubt, might undercut his own flowering confidence. Bertrand vowed that Ocker-knockerism would not threaten his crew. He would pursue a course of psychological indoctrination that would compel his men to the conviction that they were as good as, and better than, their American opponents; that as Aussies, or Ockers, whatever the label, they needed to learn arrogance, to show the world what they could do—not necessarily in an insolent, abrasive way, but with the pure inner confidence of men who know they are the best.

To achieve his goal, Bertrand resorted to some slightly unorthodox teaching methods. First he hired a combat psychologist to work with the men; then he introduced a primer lesson in the attainment of excellence, taught by a seagull named Jonathan Livingston.

The choice of a combat psychologist, rather than the traditional sports psychologist, was very deliberate. Bertrand, Bond and Jones visualized the development of a winning strategy in terms of warfare, not sport. They recruited psychologist Laurie Hayden, whose job was to focus the crew on preparing for stress, on developing self-esteem and on visualizing the mental and emotional processes they would experience when out in front of the American defender—and not, as their experience had been to date, when attempting come-from-behind victory.

Combat psychologist and helmsman pursued their mission with scientific exactitude. But Laurie Hayden's presence and his task were not met with open arms by *Australia II*'s crew. They looked askance at his reliance on psychometric testing; they felt they were being treated like human guinea pigs. Hayden's opening project was to submit all of the crew, including Bertrand, to an examination perfected at the California School of Professional Psychology. The one-hundred-and-forty-four-question test would reveal a great deal about the inner workings of the men who would sail on *Great White*. It would evaluate whether specific crew members were leaders or followers; whether their mental attitudes were those of winners or losers; whether they would be able to adjust smoothly to a brand new environment (summer in Newport, the braggadocio and swagger of Dennis Conner and the rest of the Americans). It would reveal how they would react under pressure, how much they could take, mentally and physically, without breaking.

But if crew members had a hard time accepting the

combat psychologist, Jonathan Livingston Seagull—the hero of Richard Bach's 1970s pop fable—was something else again. These men were, after all, in training to race 12-Meter yachts, to win one of the world's most coveted trophies. In the course of such an endeavor what could the fictional odyssey of a bird's quest for perfection contribute? Plenty, to John Bertrand's way of thinking. He believed in the message of the seagull as he did in Laurie Hayden's test. And the crew eventually came to prefer Jonathan Livingston. He, at least, was not threatening.

The crew learned the seagull's lesson as interpreted by John Bertrand—that there are no limits if one will only seek out perfection. They learned (feeling at first more than a little silly, until they replaced the image of the bird with their own sense of striving) how Jonathan had crashed badly into the sea coming out of a vertical dive at seventy miles an hour and then again from a ninety mile an hour try. But he kept going, turning away from the voices telling him that seagulls are supposed to be content to stay with the flock, to accept their limits. And one day he finally made a successful dive and shot above the waves—"a gray cannonball under the moon." Thereafter, the indomitable seagull progressed from one plateau of excellence to another.

By the time *Australia II*'s crew left for Newport in June of 1983, Jonathan was a kind of touchstone. The ordinary gulls dotting the sky and water at Narragansett Bay and Rhode Island Sound were constant reminders of the excellence that was within their grasp.

Through the parable of the seagull, the sessions with the combat psychologist and the constant prodding of John Bertrand, the Ocker-knocker syndrome was gradually defeated. The men reached deep within themselves, pushed themselves to the wall, and when they were flat up against that wall in exhaustion, they paused, caught their breath and went over it to another wall, and another. And when they could not push themselves any further, John Bertrand (or that damned seagull) stepped in and pushed with them, and another wall, another barrier, was overcome.

They were still pushing hard on the afternoon of September 26th; that last wall, *Red Dog*, was finally within their reach.

The American boat is bowling over the ocean ....

In the cockpit of *Great White*, seven boat lengths behind *Red Dog*, Bertrand calmly decides he must find wind. He passes the word through the boat. For the next forty minutes, the crew have one purpose: to find wind, to read wind, to harness that wind to their will. The task will not be easy. The wayward breezes of Rhode Island Sound have moderated to less than ten knots. But that is welcome news to *Australia II*, for she is more at home in light air than in fresh breeze.

Ahead, *Red Dog*'s spinnaker looks, to Bertrand's expert eye, a touch wobbly. On this downwind leg, *Red Dog* is no longer riding on the header that had saved her just minutes earlier; that windshift has finally abandoned the Americans. Dennis Conner is encountering unstable conditions and is clearly having trouble playing the tricky shifts. Bertrand bides his time. *Great White* is behaving nicely, warming to the light-moderate breezes shaping the downwind run of the final race.

Early in the summer, the Australians had described their performance on the downwind stretch as their "fifth-leg blues." For reasons at first not easily understood, the boat had performed poorly on this run. It had been the single chink in *Great White*'s armor. In a desperate attempt to solve the problem, Tom Schnackenberg and his helpers had recut and restitched sail after sail. Other boats, particularly the Italian *Azzurra* and the British *Victory '83*, had often run *Great White* down on this leg during the elimination series. Only a month earlier, *Victory '83* had temporarily checked the Australians' momentum and shocked them in the process, winning the first race of their best-of-seven semi-final having drubbed the Australians on the downwind leg. The magnitude of this single flaw of *Great White* was so great that it was thought to be a strategic trick. The Australians were accused of sandbagging downwind—deliberately misleading the Americans into thinking they were vulnerable during this vital stretch of the race.

Although the Australians vehemently denied the accusation, their fifth-leg blues mysteriously vanished. During the sixth race against the Americans, *Great White* had gained forty-six seconds on the downwind run; in the third race, she had gained an unbelievable ninety-one seconds—nine boat lengths, a gain of fifty to sixty feet for every eight hundred yards sailed, an incredible charge. In the final analysis, it did not matter whether it was Schnackenberg's recut sails or Ben Lexcen's winged keel or, as Bertrand believed, a combination of the two that eliminated the weakness. Results were what counted out on the race course, and on the downwind leg the white boat was finally delivering the desired results.

The best place in which a competitive yachtsman can find himself is called "the groove." To be in the groove is to be in a jet stream—the perfect wind tunnel. *Red Dog* had hit the groove on her marvelous fourth leg run. The beauty of such a stream of air, a header, is its constancy. The gifted helmsman never allows his boat to slip from the groove.

It is in just such a magic stream that *Great White* now suddenly finds herself. It is a tonic for Bertrand and his crew. But the course of the windstream is not marked. It is guided by unseen convections, thermals and air currents. It tends to shift to the left or the right of the race course. *Red Dog* is to the left of *Great White*. If the wind shifts to the right, the Australian boat will win the America's Cup. If it stays left, *Red Dog* will retain the coveted trophy.

In the cockpit of *Red Dog*, Dennis Conner is tense, more tense than anyone has ever seen him. Crew members are looking over their shoulders. They can tell from the full set of the Australians' spinnaker that *Great White* is feeding on a sustained breeze, that she has found the mystical groove. Navigator Halsey Herreshoff is taking ranges, measuring the distance between the boats. He confirms that the Australians are gaining, and gaining fast.

Conner's position is precarious. He steers his boat into the path of the oncoming *Great White*, trying to match her sailing angle, hoping *Red Dog*'s windshadow will disturb the air through which the Australians must sail. The tactic does not work. *Great White* gains ground relentlessly, and now the American boat needs wind the way a drowning man needs oxygen. All eyes are on the water, searching for a header. Conner cannot remain where he is and so makes a fateful decision. He believes he sees a windshift to his left, inside the track of the white boat. He jibes in the direction of the perceived wind.

At the helm of *Great White*, Bertrand observes *Red Dog*'s maneuver. The American spinnaker continues to look wobbly to him, rocking uncertainly in the unpredictable path of the wind. But his scrutiny is interrupted as he senses *Great White* falling out of the groove. The wind is shifting. Bertrand, like Conner, is confronted with a decision, a life-altering choice: left or right. He chooses right. *Great White* and *Red Dog* have agreed to disagree, and in the web of that disagreement is destiny and the America's Cup.

They do not see it ashore because they do not know what to look for.   *Hemingway*

A man who has spent the better part of his life sailing on the ocean will tell you of his nose for the wind. Perhaps there is nothing to it; perhaps "a nose for the wind" is a figment of the sailor's imagination. But you cannot tell that to a man with sailing in his blood.

John Bertrand is such a man. He inherited his nose

Great White finds the Groove

for the wind from his grandfather, Bant Cull. It was said that five minutes before a sea breeze sprang up, Bant could predict not only its arrival but its strength and direction. Just as Hemingway's Santiago, the aged fisherman, patiently shares with Manolin, the young boy, his mystical knowledge of the mysteries of the sea and the wind, of how to interpret the smell of the ocean, the formation of the clouds, the drift of the currents—so Bertrand was taught by another old man, his grandfather. Bertrand has spent his life reading these very same signs, not as a fisherman but as a yacht racer. With this lifetime on the water has come his nose for the wind, although his grandfather would have argued that he had been born with the instinct and that his years of racing had merely developed it.

The instinct has been reinforced by Rasa, Bertrand's wife. "Play the windshifts," she has said a thousand times. "Read the wind as you have always done, as only you can do." There is something mystical in her belief in his ability to smell the wind. But she has watched her husband sail on lakes and seas and oceans scattered across the face of the planet—and always, always he has found the wind.

If ever two were one, then surely we.   *Anne Bradstreet*

From the time of their marriage in 1969, Rasa and John Bertrand had lived a nomadic existence. Rasa accompanied her husband, moving from regatta to regatta, match to match, race to race: Kiel Regatta, Northern Germany (site of the Munich Olympic watersports); Admiralty's Cup, Cowes, Isle of Wight; Canada's Cup, Toronto; Kingston, Canada (site of the Montreal Olympic watersports); America's Cup, Newport

(1970, 1974, 1980 and 1983); Medemblik on the Zuider Zee, north of Amsterdam; Anzio, Southern Italy; Little Island, Finland; New Orleans; Boston; Florida; Bermuda; the Bahamas—and countless Australian regattas.

During this odyssey, the Bertrands had lived in Pawaukee, Wisconsin, in Bedford, Massachusetts, (where John obtained his master's degree in marine engineering at the Massachusetts Institute of Technology while Rasa nursed at a nearby Boston hospital, attending to drug-addicted infants born to heroin addicts); and in Australia where they lived in Sydney, Melbourne, Sun City and Perth. During this period, Rasa also raised their three children.

The summer of 1983 was Rasa Bertrand's finest hour. She was the touchstone towards which the Australian crew and their wives and companions gravitated. Her husband was the helmsman, the field commander. He would guide them in battle on the sea, while Rasa Bertrand shared her quiet, omnipresent strength on shore. She touched every crew member with a smile here, a word of encouragement there—in a unique way impossible for her husband to duplicate. She exuded confidence. She believed in *Australia II* and in John Bertrand, and with her strength and resolve this quiet woman made the crew of tough Aussie yachtsmen believe as well.

Rasa's contribution to John Bertrand's self-confidence, his steely grit, his fierce determination to win the America's Cup, was indispensable. That fundamental truth was crystallized in one confrontation midway through the final series.

Bertrand and crew were owners of a single victory, Dennis Conner and *Liberty* of three. Doubt had crept into Bertrand's heart, and that doubt was deadly. Rasa had turned to her husband, saying, *You have done no better than anyone before you.* No better than anyone before him . . . . The words, softly spoken, echoed with a devastating impact. They taunted, dared, challenged, goaded. Bertrand was not good enough; he was not matching up; he had lost the stuff of which champions are made, and he was going to have to find it.

Rasa Bertrand

Great White and Red Dog have agreed to disagree . . . .

For John Bertrand, the passage of time is elastic. There are interminable moments when the relative positions of the boats do not change, when red holds off white at arm's length. Then it

snaps back quickly—and *Great White* leaps forward, grabbing several yards from *Red Dog*.

But on this downwind leg, time is not playing
favorites. Some moments belong to the Australians, others to the Americans. Both boats give a
little, take a little; both advance and retreat. For
the men on board the competing boats and for
the men on *Fox Hunter II* and *Black Swan*, it is a
nerve-wracking business, an emotionally drain-
ing cycle of ecstasy dashed by anguish, only to be
replaced by ecstasy once again.

The anguish belongs more to the Australians
than to the Americans. Throughout the series, the
Aussies have owned the downwind leg. The last
leg is upwind, the third of the three weather legs.
Today *Red Dog* has won the previous two upwind
reaches—leg one by twenty-three seconds, leg
four by thirty-four. If *Great White* cannot catch
and pass *Liberty* on this run, the Australians will
be in a desperate situation on the final leg.

On board *Great White*, the tension is palpable,
seeming to take the form of a twelfth crew
member. He is flesh and bone, and yet he is
cadaverous. His face, the rigid mask of a man on
the edge of uncontrollable panic, is impossibly
pale, glistening with perspiration. And this ap-
parition is at once all over the boat. He stands
beside Bertrand; then in the blink of an eye he is
midship beside the winch grinders; in the same
instant he is suddenly up forward with the
bowman, hanging on for dear life as the bow of
Great White dips and rises. And then, just as
swiftly, this sure-footed phantom is back with

Bertrand. The Australian helmsman feels a hand, cold and clammy, clutch at his arm, and the touch sends a chill through his body. This is, Bertrand knows, the ultimate test of his mettle.

But then Rasa's face materializes, calm, full of confidence and strength. Without a word Rasa removes the cold, grasping hand of panic and defeat, and it disintegrates. Rasa smiles, and she too disappears; the archangel's mission has been achieved. The traitorous twelfth crew member— no, Bertrand corrects himself, the thirteenth crew member; Rasa is the twelfth—the Judas has fled.

Great White is gaining. "Can it be?" Bertrand whispers to himself. To a man, his crew stares open-mouthed at *Red Dog*, suddenly making eye contact across a scant twenty yards of foam-flecked ocean.

On *Red Dog*, heads have swiveled in disbelief. *Great White* is overtaking them, charging downwind with an awesome vengeance. The Americans are mesmerized. Man-to-man, boat-to-boat, the players are seized by a sudden paralysis. Time is frozen: *Red Dog*, *Great White*, Dennis Conner, John Bertrand, the Americans, the Australians—all form a massive living frieze.

But the frozen moment is suddenly shattered. Horrendous noise intrudes, the clatter of helicopters diving, the angry drone of hundreds of whirring propeller blades, and on the water a low-key rumble—the noise of hundreds of motor boats, their engines throbbing at low revolutions. Finally, there is the sound of the ocean breaking unmercifully against the two hulls. Only the giant silver airship far above, transmitting the scene to the world, observes the spectacle in detached silence.

Bertrand inhales deeply and releases his grip on the wheel. He focuses his attention on a single crew member, Phil Smidmore. Smidmore's *nom de guerre* is "Ya," from his habitual response to all instruction: "Yeah." He is the white boat's mastman, the crew member responsible for the clipping and unclipping of sails as they are changed. But what won him his position as part of the *Great White's* crew is instinct. Like Bertrand, Smidmore has the gift of seeing wind on water long before it betrays its presence to others.

Right now Smidmore's concentration is absolute. Again and again over the past two weeks he has been a godsend to the helmsman, unerringly guiding the white boat to wind. Most crewmen can give a helmsman guidance when the pressure is off, but when it counts, when life-and-death tension takes hold, there are few men who can step outside it and make a life-saving decision. Smidmore is such a man. He can stand at the mast, motionless as a statue, watching, watching—then call out a windshift and what it is doing, which way it is veering, a hundred yards ahead or two hundred yards or even half a mile up the track.

And now Ya is doing it again. He is reading the air and the patterns it casts on the water. He feeds his predictions to Bertrand; Bertrand sets the white boat on course. And within moments the miracle begins.

Dennis Conner does not have a Ya Smidmore on board the red boat. If any of the Americans has a nose for the wind, it is Conner himself. But instinct has disastrously escaped him this series. In 1980 with *Freedom*, he had played almost every windshift correctly; then it had been *Australia* that could not buy a shift. Now it is Conner's turn to taste bad fortune. During races five and six, he had headed to the right in search of wind, and on both occasions had been dead wrong. John Bertrand had twice gone off to the left of the course and had both times trapped a major windshift, which propelled the Australians to leads they never relinquished.

At the press conferences concluding *Red Dog*'s three victories, Conner had said "God must be an American"; at the conference in the Newport Armory following the defeats that had brought the series to a three-to-three deadlock, he had not said anything about an Australian God. It was, however, an unspoken explanation for *Great White*'s victories.

God an Australian? It was a blasphemous, traitorous notion that brought to mind the unthinkable: America might lose the Cup. It was a flashback to the time, one hundred and thirty-two years ago, when an entire empire thought that God was an Englishman, and a Yankee schooner named *America* had cast grave doubts on that belief, off Cowes on the Isle of Wight.

Above the maelstrom of noise, Conner can identify only one sound: the intense pounding of *Great White*'s bow crashing through the waves. He has to do something and so, in search of the windshifts the white boat has been finding as if by magic, he begins to jibe, to maneuver the boat back and forth. But a jibe is a gamble in which time is the wager. Each jibe costs Conner about five seconds—half a boat length.

Downwind Charge

On the ocean race course, as at the gaming table, there is both a conservative and a risky way to play. The payoff on the conservative moves is marginal; on the bold, audacious moves, the payoff can be outstanding—or the loss devastating. At the start-line, Conner usually goes for the high-risk move and, because of his talent, normally wins. But as the race wears on, the tactics he uses in the search for elusive windshifts tend to be more conservative. Now, however, he has been forced from that careful wagering. He has to gamble.

In his desperate search for air on this leg, Conner jibes eleven times. Eleven times the wind spins and hovers around him, and every time it settles in the wrong place. Conner cannot seem to pick the winning number, to find the wind. *Great White* jibes only five times and repeatedly, unerringly, finds fresh wind on each shift. The difference between the two competitors is that the Australians are relying, not on the gambler's instincts, but on a nose for the wind.

The two boats are on opposite sides of the race course, with the marker buoy a short distance ahead of them. Now *Red Dog* and *Great White* must once again converge, go around the buoy and sail upwind on the final weather leg to the finish line, where destiny awaits them.

On *Fox Hunter II*, faces are grim. These great yachtsmen, all of them winners, know the cruel truth: *Red Dog* will trail *Great White* before the combatants round the America's Cup buoy. The only question is: By how much will she fall behind?

On board *Black Swan*, by contrast, faces are relieved, joyous. Ben Lexcen and Tom Schnackenberg have returned from below deck not quite sure whether to believe this swift change of fortune. They stand together with Alan Bond and Warren Jones. Their boat is now sailing as it has in their most enchanted dreams.

Beneath the giant, pristine white spinnaker, Bertrand and his crew look like small, insignificant creatures—insects clinging to a water-logged piece of wood. Yet, they are the heart and soul of their craft, of their ethereal cloud of sail. Bond, Jones, Lexcen and Schnackenberg are the shoreguard. They are separated by more than ocean from Bertrand and his band of brothers; for on board *Great White*, as it powers toward the America's Cup buoy, is the rarest form of *esprit de corps*, the kind found only in the height of battle. The men in the shoreguard, proud and excited as they are, cannot feel the same; they would gladly give anything to be on board *Australia II* as she passes *Liberty*.

4:22pm

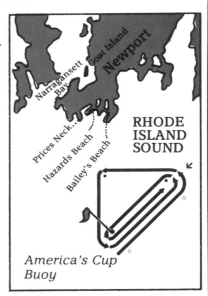

RHODE
ISLAND
SOUND

Narragansett
Bay

Goat Island

Newport

Prices Neck

Hazards Beach

Bailey's Beach

*America's Cup
Buoy*

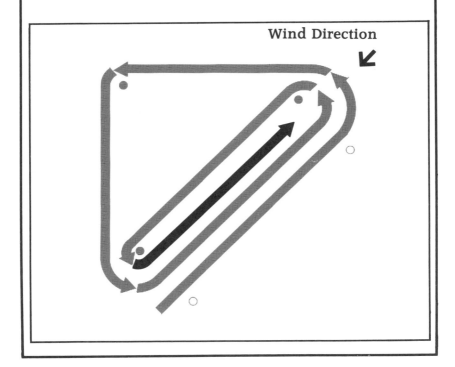

Wind Direction

The Sixth Leg

Victory at all costs, victory in spite of all terror, victory however long and hard the road may be.

Churchill

At the New York Yacht Club on West 44th Street, late arrivals are being seated for luncheon. The hushed, restrained atmosphere belies the fact that the club is but one hundred and fifty miles from Newport, from the brilliant sun and sky and the life-and-death struggle taking place on the waters of Rhode Island Sound. There is not the fever pitch of excitement that might be expected considering the outcome is as important to the occupants of this elegant building as it is to the eleven men toiling on board *Liberty*. If the diners are at all swept up in the fate of their standard-bearer, it is a sentiment to which the casual observer is not privy. Perhaps the reticent demeanor of the members is a natural offshoot of the haughty and solemn surroundings. The proper decorum of the New York Yacht Club does not permit public displays of emotion, however deeply those emotions might be felt.

These men (women make up only a tiny minority of

the membership) are the very powerful and the very privileged of American society. To gain admission to this bastion of yesteryear—the traditions of the Club are modeled after one of London's famous nineteenth-century Pall Mall gentlemen's clubs—remains a singular achievement. Perhaps surprisingly, ownership of a yacht is not a prerequisite for membership. A prospective candidate must, however, manifest some degree of interest in matters maritime. And yacht owners do enjoy preferential status among members; only they may vote on club business. Club membership hovers at the twenty-six hundred mark, of which approximately one half own yachts. To belong, one must be nominated and seconded and then have three other club members provide letters of recommendation.

The New York Yacht Club has been at its mid-Manhattan location since 1901. The solid granite edifice jutting out over the pavement of West 44th Street like the transom of a Spanish galleon was given to the club by turn-of-the-century financier J. Pierpont Morgan, a yachting enthusiast and one of a long line of power-brokers (others have included such notables as Cornelius Vanderbilt and August Belmont) who has belonged to the club since its inception in 1844.

Stepping inside the club, the visitor feels as though he has entered the spacious and luxurious quarters of an Admiral of the Fleet. From one of the comfortable overstuffed chairs he can survey the decor, which is nautical throughout. The showplace is the Model Room, where memorabilia from one hundred and thirty-two years of America's Cup campaigns are displayed. Inside glass cases are models of the yachts that have challenged and defended, a *corps d'élite* guaranteed to quicken the member's pulse—for these champions (*Columbia, Ranger, Intrepid, Courageous, Freedom*) recall victory after glorious victory. But shrine-like as it is, this room is not the shrine. The lustrous America's Cup is in the Trophy Room where, because so many have come over the years to see her—to reflect on all that she represents for the New York Yacht Club and for America—the carpet is threadbare, a footpath fashioned by pilgrims.

On this late-September day in 1983, the silver Cup shines as brightly as ever from her place of honor in the Trophy Room. But some of the latecomers settling down to lunch sense impending doom. Before entering the Dining Room, they have paid brief homage to their beloved Cup, stealing a glimpse in what may be a silent farewell.

To the north, on Rhode Island Sound, the battle rages; yet strangely there is no up-to-the-minute word on how Dennis Conner and *Liberty* are faring. For true to the New York Yacht Club's determination not to let the modern world encroach on its traditions of a century and more, the club is not possessed of a single radio or television. The news, when it finally arrives, comes from a rather unlikely source: a bricklayer, a member of a construction crew making repairs to the building. This gentleman has brought a radio to work, and at the conclusion of each leg, he surfaces from the basement with a report. The updates are posted on a bulletin board. The latest bulletin is as terse as it is foreboding: "Fifth mark, *Australia II* by twenty-one seconds."

A hemisphere away from the sun over Rhode Island Sound and from the somber twilight of the New York Yacht Club's inner sanctum, darkness reigns. The sky Down Under is a perfect indigo in which blazes the Southern Cross, the awe-inspiring constellation that dominates the Australian firmament. In the deserts and featureless expanses of the Great Outback, sacred hunting ground of the aborigine, there is no boundary between heaven and earth. The Cross seems to have fallen from the sky; its star-suns burn in the blackness like brilliant but distant campfires.

But the stillness and silence of night on the Great Outback does not extend to the Royal Perth Yacht Club—located less than an hour's drive from the start of the barren heartland of Australia.

The Royal Perth rests on the shore of the Swan River at Pelican Point, a small, sandy scrub-bush peninsula. The building is whitewashed and cubist, all stark surfaces and right angles. There is no illusion here of the grandeur of a Spanish galleon or of *belle époque* architecture. At the same time, however, the Mediterranean flavor is wholly incongruous with the architectural heritage of Perth itself, which is evocative of the pastoral charm of an English village.

A few miles up the Swan, modern Perth rises in crystalline air like the skyline of Phoenix, Arizona, or to the eye of many Americans of an earlier generation, a young Los Angeles. Perth is a dynamic metropolis of just over a million people; although it possesses something of Southern California's laid-back ambience, it is also an aggressive, frontier-style city, a place of limitless ambition and golden promise.

The Indian Ocean is a shore breeze away from Perth. It is, after Chicago and Wellington, New Zealand, the world's windiest city. It is also blessed with an inordinate amount of sunshine. Put wind, sun and ocean together in the same quadrant and a sailor's paradise emerges—a paradise from which *Great White* had sailed.

The cachet of the Royal Perth is not old money. It is not given to stuffiness or the stiff formalities and protocol of the New York Yacht Club. There is naturally a social ladder, but the climb is not nearly as narrow or as exhausting as that found in New York. Armed with bold ambition, one can reach the uppermost rungs of the Royal Perth almost overnight. Class distinction is rarely an impediment. The Royal Perth tends, therefore, to attract a younger, less sophisticated membership.

At the Royal Perth, there is no prohibition against televisions, radios and other twentieth-century wizardry. While in New York news of the race reaches the members by a circuitous and antiquated route, members and guests at the Royal Perth are glued to virtually instant video images of the contest. A boisterous party is in progress, in marked contrast to the almost funereal atmosphere at the New York Yacht Club. The Australians are jubilant: They are imbued with a sense of imminent victory. Already they have done what no other challenger has done before—pushed the series to a seventh, sudden-death race. They have badly beaten the Americans in three races and gained an unheard-of lead in an aborted fourth. But now the noisy overflow Aussie crowd lusts for more Yankee blood. They want *Great White* to crush *Red Dog* in one final humiliation and deliver the America's Cup to their modest clubhouse at the bottom of the world.

God an Australian?

The late afternoon light is gradually fading; the sky grows a deeper blue and the ocean darkens. *Australia II*'s sails rise into the heavens, pyramids of luminous gold and amber. On the western and northern horizons, the Rhode Island coastline is a shadowy charcoal smudge, and to the south and east a thin glowing band of magenta straddles the length of the ocean horizon. In the foreground of this horizon, four and a half miles from *Liberty* and the white boat, is *Black Knight* and, opposite her, a six-foot-high orange pylon marker. An invisible finish line is strung between boat and marker. Within an hour, either *Great White* or *Red Dog* will be first to cross that line and claim the America's Cup.

John Bertrand is not, like his countrymen halfway around the world, in the throes of elation. He is, despite his twenty-one-second lead, uneasy. He is having trouble steering. The spectator chop is playing rough with the boat; the hull feels as if it is being pummeled by a tireless boxer. Punch after punch is thrown by short, steep waves. And to complicate matters the wind is falling, the sails are weakening, boat speed is dropping. The hunt for wind continues. The race is far from over.

Bertrand is acutely aware that *Red Dog* is still very much alive, still dangerous. He is certain that at the beginning of this leg Conner will display a defensive posture, despite being behind by two boat lengths. The American will attempt to find the same upwind shifts that propelled him to good leads in the first two weather legs. But the sea breeze continues to be moderate, blowing now at six to seven knots. Wind conditions are shaping up nicely in favor of *Great White*. And Bertrand has no intention of letting Conner escape the white boat's windshadow. Once Conner discovers that he cannot gain boat speed in the light air now prevailing on the Sound, the American will have but one option: to initiate a tacking duel that, Bertrand knows, will be vicious.

For ten minutes the boats sail on as Bertrand has predicted, Conner searching desperately for a windshift. But it is not to be. There are four miles to cover to gain *Black Knight* and the finish: forty minutes in this light air. Dennis Conner has run out of options. He must tack if he is to get out from behind *Great White* and find wind of his own.

The sun is sinking into the western horizon, casting a fiery red shadow over the sea. The light glints off the red boat onto the water sliding swiftly beneath its hull. To airborne observers, it appears as if *Liberty* is trailing blood on the ocean.

Bertrand anticipates Conner's do-or-die maneuver. If the American tacks, Bertrand will have to do the same, to keep *Red Dog* from escaping his windshadow. A tacking duel will test his crew's strength and stamina. It will also subject *Great White* to unprecedented stress; her one major flaw is that she is subject to equipment failure. During races one and two, both American victories, the Australian boat had suffered major gear problems. But since then, *Great White* has performed superbly.

"I have nothing to offer but blood, toil, tears and sweat." Churchill's words ring in Bertrand's ears. He is preparing to deliver them to his winch grinders: Chink Longley, Splash Richardson and Peter Costello. These are the big men, the defensive linemen, of a 12-Meter. Their toil and sweat will change the boat's course again and again in the desperate final duel.

Conner abruptly throws the first tack at the Australian boat. The maneuver has none of the balletic grace associated with yacht racing. It is a move carefully choreographed, but its essence is brawn. Each time the boat tacks, the giant mainsail and mast boom swing to the opposite side of the hull. The winch grinders must move this massive wall of pressure, fractional inch by fractional inch, harnessing the force of the wind.

Tacking! The warning is suddenly screamed. The boom is released. It swings across the deck in

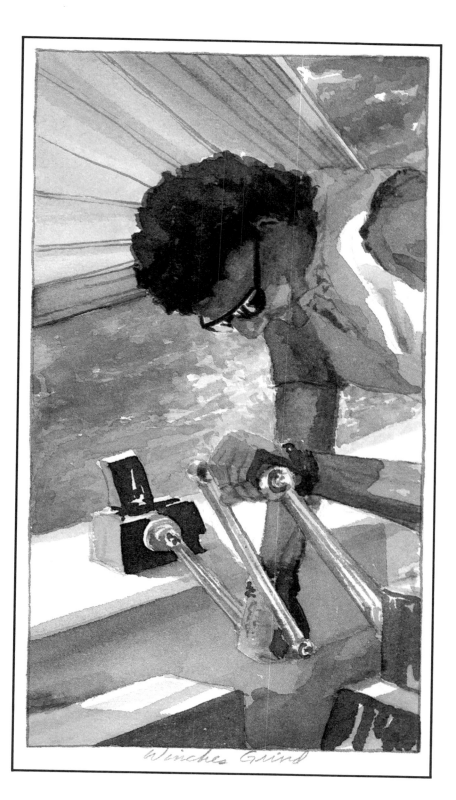

Winches Grind

a vicious cross-cut. The mainsail shudders, the hull shudders, *Great White* shudders. The mainsail is trapped. The grinders begin to propel their muscular arms as a cyclist furiously pumps his legs. Their hands are thick with calluses and scars from untold numbers of cuts; gloves offer only slight protection.

Tack after tack is thrown and still *Red Dog* is held back by *Great White*. The men on each boat can hear the other's winches grinding, a primitive gnashing of teeth. The boats are two creatures locked in a life-and-death struggle.

The grinders' hearts are pounding at three times their normal rate. The men are soaked in perspiration and sea water. They have lost all sense of the number of tacks they have made. But Bertrand and Conner and the millions of spectators have not: twenty-five.

Incredibly, *Red Dog* is winning this grueling duel. Tack by tack, it is creeping up on *Great White*. Bertrand can hear the angry, growling machinery of Conner's boat stealing closer.

Dennis Conner now does the completely unexpected: He fakes tacks like a boxer feigning punches. The strategy pays immediate dividends, rattling the already frayed nerves of *Great White*'s crew. Now the cry on board *Australia II* is *Tack! No! No! Don't go! Wait . . . tack! Tack! Tack! Tack the boat! No, hold it!* It is a hair-raising, nervewracking series of commands and counter commands. And all the time, inch by hard-fought inch, *Red Dog* is narrowing the gap.

The tacks now number in the thirties. On board *Fox Hunter II*, there is a desperate hope; on *Black Swan*, there is dismay: Could fate be this grotesque, this cruel?

Bertrand is under attack and he must do something. His boat's tacking is becoming ragged, uncoordinated—a development that must be corrected. Rapidly he assesses *Great White*'s situation. He still has boat speed on *Red Dog*. He has been trapped into a tacking duel; yet *Australia II* is the superior tacking boat. It is his crew, rather than the boat itself, that is faltering. The colossal pressure is getting to his men.

He can now hear *Red Dog*'s winches as clearly as his own. He can even hear the excited voices of the Americans. *Red Dog* is nipping at his heels. He suddenly experiences a second bout of split-second flashbacks: 1976, the East German's eyes and the humiliating capsizing of his Finn-racer; 1980, Dennis Conner's triumphant eyes after thrashing *Australia*; and Rasa . . . Rasa . . . *You've done no better than the rest* . . . . By God, that he had done . . . *Let your natural talents flow* . . . . Christ, that he is *not* doing. He is on the verge of catastrophic eleventh-hour collapse. He is facing the danger the combat psychologist had supposedly inoculated the crew against: panic. Now, however, it is not the psychologist's teachings that begin to dominate his thoughts; it is Rasa . . . . *Relax, John let your natural talents flow* . . . . and Bertrand finds himself relaxing with a swiftness that surprises him. His mind is focused absolutely on the problem at hand. The command to relax is passed from man to man.

Bertrand brings the tacking battle to an abrupt halt. He has a boat length on *Red Dog*; he has boat speed. He needs a windshift to deliver the knockout blow to Conner and the Americans. And within a minute, as if by divine appointment, *Australia II* meets a freshening shift.

The Australians, with sublime grace and power, pull effortlessly away from the Americans. It is, for all held spellbound by the moment—those in the Goodyear blimp, in the helicopters and airplanes, in the press boat, in *Black Swan* and *Fox Hunter II*, in the spectator fleet now encircling the last stretch of the race course, and for the entire population of a continent twelve thousand miles away—the *coup de grâce*.

On *Red Dog* the grinders are bathed in blood, toil, sweat and now, at the moment of judgment, in tears. Fighting for breath, drawing from a well of strength and endurance they did not know they possessed, they had thrown forty-seven tacks—over a period of less than thirty minutes—at *Great White*. They had clawed their way into striking range and now the wind—the goddamn traitorous wind—has whisked the prey out of their desperate grasp. They stand or crouch or kneel in exhaustion and stupefaction. There is *Black Knight* sitting serenely on the ocean; but suddenly they can no longer see her or the finish line. They can see only *Australia II*, the hated *Great White*, her sails golden as she catches the light of a glorious setting sun. She is triumphant: a vision of victory and destiny.

It is over. *Red Dog* and Dennis Conner have lost the America's Cup.

A Second Shot Rang Out

A Second Shot Rang Out

The Australian story is something like a fun fair . . . . Ferris wheels go round and round, hurdy-gurdies grind out the same tunes . . . . Apart from the showmen no one seems more important than anyone else. What is the purpose of it all? How can a fun fair give a young nation an inspiring history?

Douglas Pike

A second shot rang out over Rhode Island Sound on September 26, 1983. Four hours, fifteen minutes after the first cannon roar, the second—fired from the deck of *Black Knight*—proclaimed *Australia II*'s victory. Forty-one seconds later *Liberty* crossed the finish line.

In Australia a new day had already dawned, and the entire nation jumped to its feet, arms reaching for the sky in triumph. The unrestrained emotion was unlike anything the country had experienced before; it even surpassed VJ Day, the end of World War II in the Pacific. The attempt to win the America's Cup had become a test of Australian nationhood. Every Ocker, from parliamentarians in Canberra to opal miners in White Cliffs, to sheep station owners on the periphery of the Great Outback, had engaged the foe—the defenders of the America's Cup. And so it was not only John Bertrand and crew that exulted in victory—Australians everywhere celebrated.

An article in the Australian edition of *Time*—written from the heart, Aussie style—captured the fiercely emotional and patriotic mood of the country following *Australia II*'s victory in the third race of the series: "No challenger had ever won more than two races, but that is merely a statistic. What was on display in Newport was nobility. The Australians showed technological brilliance, consummate sailing skill, luck, intuition, nerve, courage, stamina and fanatic determination to win. It also took millions of dollars on both sides . . . the price of admission in 12-Meter yacht racing. But no amount of money could have bought what Aussie guts and gall have won to date."

By the time of the final race even Donald Horne, Australia's arch-pragmatist and cynical author of *The Lucky Country*, was swept up in the euphoria: "After a few minutes of watching the yachts' mutual tacking—which seemed, in both their self-absorption and in their fragility and uncertainty, to be a long shared caress—I found myself gripped with a greedy yearning that it would be our side that would win . . . . And when, victorious, they played *Advance Australia Fair*, I again had this humiliating experience of wanting to cry."

At the Royal Perth Yacht Club, there were tears on many a face, tears of relief and of unbridled elation. It was 4:20 a.m. on the Australian west coast, and the party that had been ebbing and flowing with *Great White*'s leg-by-leg performance on the race course erupted into tumult. Every bottle of champagne was uncorked and revellers stood beneath a drenching shower of golden wine. The Australian Prime Minister, Bob Hawke, arrived to announce an unofficial holiday for the country. "Any employer who sacks a man today," he proclaimed (sputtering momentarily under a fountain of champagne), "is a bum!" Behind him fanatics waved a banner featuring a kangaroo pummeling an American eagle.

New York
Yacht Club

The feelings of the nation were reflected in the headlines. "Attention all stations. The Eagle has been plucked," proclaimed a typical one. (Headlines in the United States, meanwhile, were mournful: "America's Cup to Australia II . . . one hundred and thirty-two years of U.S. reign ends" said The *New York Times*. The *Washington Post* was equally solemn: "Liberty falters and now it's Australia's Cup.")

The most gloating proclamations belonged, oddly, not to the Australian press but to the British—still smarting more than a century after their loss to *America*. The London *Daily Mail*'s correspondent in Newport, under a headline that crowed "Magic Matilda!" stated with unconcealed delight: "It happened, and it happened in the manner of lurid fiction. *Australia II* sailed back from the dead sea here last night to beat *Liberty*, to win the America's Cup . . . . They won a four-and-a-half-hour race by precisely forty-one seconds, as America watched in helpless agony."

In fact, a large part of America was not watching at all. The late-September U.S. sports calendar was crowded with a multitude of competitions; the National Football

League season had begun, while professional basketball and hockey were concluding their pre-season schedules. And pennant fever was in the air as the baseball season drew to a close and the World Series approached. *Australia II*'s remarkable upset, therefore, was reported on sports broadcasts in an almost desultory, off-hand manner.

But within the confines of the New York Yacht Club, the tense news reports sounded like a death knell. The bedside vigil was over; the America's Cup was lost. As at the Royal Perth, tears flowed freely and so, ironically, did champagne. One club member appeared with a bottle and, after a brief statement that was really a eulogy, poured the contents into the Cup—forgetting that it had no bottom. It was an awkward, maudlin moment but, at the same time, a rather fitting conclusion to the day and to an entire summer of misadventure for the New York Yacht Club.

The Cup was quickly cleaned up and placed in its three-quarter-inch-thick black plywood box. Shortly before eight o'clock—less than three hours after *Australia II* had crossed the finish line—the box was loaded onto a Brink's truck for the one hundred and fifty mile journey north to Newport. It was a wrenching moment for club members. Across the street, a group of fifty or so Australian supporters broke into a loud and forceful rendition of the country's folk anthem, *Waltzing Matilda*.

In Newport, that same song greeted the Australian heroes as their boat was towed into the harbor. The scene on the waterfront was chaos. Night had fallen, but the sky was bright from the glare of television lights set

up dockside and from the overhead starburst of exploding firecrackers.

As she towed *Australia II*, the tender boat, *Black
Swan*, had to fight for every inch of headway. The harbor
was packed with hundreds of spectator craft, all eager to
bask in reflected glory. Landlubbers were elbow-to-
elbow dockside, also desperate to be a part of this extraordinary and historic moment.

Towards the end of tow-in, John Bertrand sur-
rendered the helm to Ben Lexcen, the man whose genius
had given birth to *Great White*. Lexcen, wearing a smile
almost as bright as one of the klieg lights trained on his
face, steered his creation the last hundred yards to
Newport Offshore. Alan Bond—the Australian migrant
who, by unwavering dedication, had transformed his
ultimate dream into reality—hopscotched from *Black
Swan* to an inflatable dinghy to *Australia II*. He was accompanied by syndicate executive Warren Jones and
sailmaker Tom Schnackenberg.

While skyrockets exploded overhead, now and then
eclipsed by clouds of green-and-gold balloons, and
spotlights bathed *Great White* in silver-white glare,
these men stood in the cockpit of their champion,
unabashedly exchanging tearful bear hugs. This was
their moment of glory; they had reached the summit of
their mountain, a mountain that had taken Bond and
his team more than a decade to conquer. *They had won
the America's Cup.* The realization was just beginning to
sink in. It had not yet taken hold of their lives; that
would happen in the days and weeks to come. But no
other post-victory moment could equal this one.

One other person who belonged to this group was
Rasa Bertrand. Finally making her way through the

pandemonium to her husband's side on *Australia II*, she sobbed uncontrollably while he hugged her for long moments. The emotions of fourteen years of pilgrimage, a journey filled with adversity, labor and love, finally spilled out.

And John Bertrand? He remained somewhat dazed, knowing he had triumphed but unable, as yet, to comprehend the enormity of that victory. As the white boat glided across the finish line, he had found himself in the arms of Hugh Treharne, his tactician, sobbing, like Rasa, in release from the enormous pressure under which he had been living. He was a man who, like Alan Bond, had taken a dream and made it come true. Whatever other chapters he might write in his life's story, nothing would compare with his moment of shining glory, 5:20:45 p.m. on the afternoon of September 26, 1983—the instant at which he had been the first challenger to win the America's Cup.

There is rarely glory in defeat, and Dennis Conner sought none. Conner's down-to-earth creed—"No excuse to lose"—forbade ruminations on his gallant defense of the America's Cup. From *Liberty*, Conner made his way across an improvised footbridge of pleasure craft to *Australia II*. He found John Bertrand and clasped the victorious Australian's hand in congratulation.

It was an awkward moment for both men. Almost immediately, the American helmsman left *Great White* for the Newport Armory and his final press conference of the summer. There, eyes red-rimmed, cheeks tear-stained, voice on the edge of cracking, he spoke quietly and simply: "Today *Australia II* was just a better boat. And they beat us. And we have no excuses. So I'd like at this point to congratulate Alan Bond and *Australia II* on their superb effort over the summer. They proved they were an outstanding boat and today was their day."

His duty done, Conner disappeared into the crowded Newport night, hand in hand with his wife, Judy, who had been his steadfast partner throughout the ordeal of the twenty-fifth defense. The following day, the Conners left for San Diego.

Dennis Conner's absence from the brief but sunstruck Marble House ceremony at which the Cup was officially presented to the Royal Perth Yacht Club, on the day of his departure from Newport, garnered him criticism from the Australians; they perceived it as lack of sportsmanship. Meanwhile, the New York Yacht Club's Cup committee did not even bother to extend a formal thank-you to Conner for his heroic effort to keep the Cup in America.

John Bertrand and company spent a few more days in the United States. The Australian helmsman made an unofficial visit to the New York Yacht Club, during which he entered the Trophy Room and stood on the threadbare carpet before the spot where the America's Cup had rested for so many years. That personal pilgrimage completed, Bertrand departed for his homeland, there to be greeted by the adulation reserved for a conquering hero.

It was a reminder of John Cox Stevens' triumphant return to America in 1851. Bertrand and Stevens stood at opposite ends of a bridge of time spanning one hundred and thirty-two years; but they stood as equals. They shared a prize that symbolized their nations' pride, honor and aspirations—the ungainly Victorian ewer that is the America's Cup.

The America's Cup

The United States has to move very fast to even stand still.
John Fitzgerald Kennedy

The visitor to the Royal Perth Yacht Club is greeted by a uniformed commissionaire, a veteran of the Australian armed forces. Permission to view the America's Cup is granted without fuss. The only injunction—"No photographs, please"—is politely spoken. Directions to the Cup are equally succinct: "Straight up the stairs." The visitor is then left to his own devices. The informality contrasts sharply with the formal protocol of a visit to the venerable New York Yacht Club; when the Cup resided in Manhattan, one could see it only by appointment. But Alan Bond had declared in Newport that if his syndicate were to win the Cup, it would be accessible to one and all. He and the Royal Perth Yacht Club have kept that promise.

Straight up the stairs—two flights—and the visitor finds himself in a small boardroom. The walls are covered in plain beige wallpaper; the only furnishings are an ordinary office table and plain black vinyl chairs. It is not the kind of room in which one expects to find one of the world's most famous trophies. But in one corner, an alcove has been constructed. Inside, mounted on a marble pedestal and gleaming against a background of scarlet cloth, is the America's Cup. The visitor and the Cup are separated by a glass partition. The symbol of yacht racing supremacy—and of a nation's pride—is highlighted by the beams of two spotlights, which burn on the highly polished silver with such brilliance that the visitor is at first forced to avert his eyes, as if his gaze had accidentally wandered to a blazing desert sun.

The Cup itself—ugly, ill-proportioned, overwrought as it is—has an undeniable presence, an aura that is almost magical. It enchants, not by graceful rendering of line and form or by genius of interpretation and expression, but by what it represents: dreams and ambitions that go far beyond the suffocating grasp of the ordinary, that take direct aim on the impossible.

After several moments of silent contemplation, the visitor's eyes drift to a collection of photographs that grace a wall immediately to the right of the Cup. Five of the six photographs feature, as might be expected, *Australia II* and *Liberty* during their climactic encounter on Rhode Island Sound. But the sixth and largest photograph is a close-up of the grim faces of the New York Yacht Club's America's Cup committee, the photo snapped at the instant *Great White* crossed the finish line. The transparent grief of these proud men stands out in stark relief. The photograph seems meant to remind the Royal Perth Yacht Club, and all who visit this Trophy Room, that the New York Yacht Club was, and remains, the enemy.

If the American yacht racing establishment, and the New York Yacht Club in particular, required an extra push to encourage an all-out attempt to recapture the Cup, a moment studying this photograph would serve the purpose. In fact, so deep were the wounds from the bitter and protracted controversies of the summer of 1983 that a good number of New York Yacht Club members were in favor of not mounting a challenge for the Cup in Australia. The sentiment that *Australia II* was an illegal mutant and had bested *Liberty* by skullduggery rather than fair play was widespread, a sentiment reminiscent of British reaction toward *America*'s 1851 victory—that John Cox Stevens' yacht had triumphed by nefarious means and not by superior design and seamanship.

But ultimately the New York Yacht Club's attitude underwent a transformation, as had the Royal Yacht Squadron's, belatedly and grudgingly, a century and a half ago. The wrong could be righted on another day, on

Royal Perth
Yacht Club

another race course. To that end, the New York Yacht Club has committed itself wholeheartedly—as have five other American syndicates and challengers from Canada, England, France, Italy and New Zealand.

When the challenge trials begin off Perth for the first Australian defense, commencing in October, 1986, Dennis Conner will not be at the helm of the New York Yacht Club's boat, *America II*. That honor will go to John Kolius, the unassuming Texan who tested Conner's and *Liberty*'s mettle in 1983 with *Courageous*. Conner will return to America's Cup competition as skipper of *Stars and Stripes*, the challenger from his native San Diego Yacht Club. Tom Blackaller, who also lost the chance to defend the Cup in 1983 to Conner, will challenge under the aegis of San Francisco's St. Francis Yacht Club. Designer Johan Valentijn returns with his latest creation, *Eagle*, competing under the auspices of the Newport Harbor Yacht Club.

Familiar names also appear in the roster of Australian boats and syndicates that will be competing for the opportunity to defend the Cup during the final series in February of 1987. Alan Bond and Warren Jones head the America's Cup Defense 1987 syndicate out of the Royal Perth Yacht Club; their boat will be either *Australia III* or *Australia IV*, both yachts designed by—who else?—Ben Lexcen. Lexcen has also designed another potential defender, the Royal South Australia Yacht Squadron's *South Australia*. Sir James Hardy, the man who skippered *Australia* in the 1980 America's Cup challenge and who played a prominent role in *Australia II*'s success, is providing training assistance to this syndicate.

One man who will not be returning to the America's Cup wars, however, is John Bertrand. His victory on Rhode Island Sound bestowed upon him the status of national hero—modern Australia's first. This achievement, wrought by vision, perseverance and sacrifice, is Bertrand's legacy to his country and to those who would vie for the America's Cup.

But John Bertrand's quest for the Cup was not motivated by hunger for glory. His challenge was a personal one. Yet, woven within the cloth of his odyssey is the inspiration of two individuals: Nan Cull, his grandmother, and Tom Pearkes, his great-great grandfather, who worked with Sir Thomas Lipton on the illustrious *Shamrock*s, yachts which valiantly, but in vain, challenged for the Cup five times. On September 26, 1983, John Bertrand joined hands across the years with his grandmother and his great-great grandfather and closed a circle on a dream and on that ungainly Victorian trophy known to the world as the America's Cup.

All that is and shall be,
And all the past, is his.

Sophocles

Appendices

The Round-Robin Eliminations

Yacht	Club	Round Robin A		Round Robin B		Round Robin C	
		Won	Lost	Won	Lost	Won	Lost
Australia II	Royal Perth Yacht Club	11	1	10	2	15	1
Victory '83	Royal Burnham Yacht Club	8	4	7	5	10	6
Azzurra	Yacht Club Costa Smeralda	5	7	7	5	9	7
Canada I	Secret Cove Yacht Club	4	8	6	6	9	7
Challenge 12	Royal Yacht Club of Victoria	10	2	7	5	7	9
France III	Yacht Club de France	4	8	2	10	2	10
Advance	Royal Sydney Yacht Squadron	0	12	2	10	0	12

TWENTY-FIFTH DEFENSE

GAIN: LEG-BY-LEG

RACE	ONE	TWO	THREE	FOUR	FIVE	SIX	SEVEN
DATE	SEPT. 14	SEPT. 15	SEPT. 17	SEPT. 20	SEPT. 21	SEPT. 23	SEPT. 26
LEG: WEATHER	0.08	0.45	1.14	0.36	0.23	2.29	0.29
POWER	0.02	0.14	0.22	0.12	0.00	0.19	0.16
POWER	0.26	0.10	0.10	0.00	0.50	1.18	0.22
WEATHER	0.13	1.09	0.33	0.00	0.53	0.24	0.34
DOWNWIND	0.06	0.17	1.32	0.11	0.19	0.46	1.18
WEATHER	0.35	1.02	0.28	0.08	0.55	0.43	0.20

Australia II   Liberty

Roll Call of Honor

Record of the America's Cup Matches

Name	Country of Origin	Sponsoring Club
	1851	
America	U.S.	New York Yacht Club
	First Defense—1870	
Magic	U.S.	New York Yacht Club
Cambria	England	Royal Thames
	Second Defense—1871	
Columbia	U.S.	New York Yacht Club
Livonia	England	Royal Harwich
	Third Defense—1876	
Madeleine	U.S.	New York Yacht Club
Countess of	Canada	Royal Canadian
Dufferin		
	Fourth Defense—1881	
Mischief	U.S.	New York Yacht Club
Atlanta	Canada	Bay of Quinte
	Fifth Defense—1885	
Puritan	U.S.	New York Yacht Club
Genesta	England	Royal Yacht Squadron
	Sixth Defense—1886	
Mayflower	U.S.	New York Yacht Club
Galatea	England	Royal Northern
	Seventh Defense—1887	
Volunteer	U.S.	New York Yacht Club
Thistle	Scotland	Royal Clyde

	Eighth Defense—1893	
Vigilant	U.S.	New York Yacht Club
Valkyrie II	England	Royal Yacht Squadron

	Ninth Defense—1895	
Defender	U.S.	New York Yacht Club
Valkyrie III	England	Royal Yacht Squadron

	Tenth Defense—1899	
Columbia	U.S.	New York Yacht Club
Shamrock	Ireland	Royal Ulster

	Eleventh Defense—1901	
Columbia	U.S.	New York Yacht Club
Shamrock II	Ireland	Royal Ulster

	Twelfth Defense—1903	
Reliance	U.S.	New York Yacht Club
Shamrock III	Ireland	Royal Ulster

	Thirteenth Defense—1920	
Resolute	U.S.	New York Yacht Club
Shamrock IV	Ireland	Royal Ulster

	Fourteenth Defense—1930	
Enterprise	U.S.	New York Yacht Club
Shamrock V	Ireland	Royal Ulster

	Fifteenth Defense—1934	
Rainbow	U.S.	New York Yacht Club
Endeavour	England	Royal Yacht Squadron

	Sixteenth Defense—1937	
Ranger	U.S.	New York Yacht Club
Endeavour II	England	Royal Yacht Squadron

	Seventeenth Defense—1958	
Columbia	U.S.	New York Yacht Club
Sceptre	England	Royal Yacht Squadron

	Eighteenth Defense—1962	
Weatherly	U.S.	New York Yacht Club
Gretel	Australia	Royal Sydney

	Nineteenth Defense—1964	
Constellation	U.S.	New York Yacht Club
Sovereign	England	Royal Thames

	Twentieth Defense—1967	
Intrepid	U.S.	New York Yacht Club
Dame Pattie	Australia	Royal Sydney

	Twenty-first Defense—1970	
Intrepid	U.S.	New York Yacht Club
Gretel II	Australia	Royal Sydney

	Twenty-second Defense—1974	
Courageous	U.S.	New York Yacht Club
Southern Cross	Australia	Royal Perth

	Twenty-third Defense—1977	
Courageous	U.S.	New York Yacht Club
Australia	Australia	Sun City

	Twenty-fourth Defense—1980	
Freedom	U.S.	New York Yacht Club
Australia	Australia	Royal Perth

	Twenty-fifth Defense—1983	
Australia II	Australia	Royal Perth
Liberty	U.S.	New York Yacht Club

Schooner

Cutter

J. Boat   12-Meter

Two-masted schooners beginning with *America* were used in the early years of America's Cup competition. In the 1880s much larger, single-masted cutters became popular. J-Boats, first raced in 1930, were smaller but swifter than their predecessors. The even smaller but more maneuverable 12-Meters came into use in 1958.

About the Author

Mark Clark has written two law texts for McGraw-Hill. He is also the author of *JETSET: The North Atlantic Route*, an air traveler's companion to Europe; and of two forthcoming books featuring travel to the South Seas and the Far East.

Mark Clark lives in Kingston, Ontario with his wife and two children.